Appomattox

Christopher Hampton was born in the Azores in 1946. He wrote his first play, *When Did You Last See My Mother?*, at the age of eighteen. Since then, his plays have included *The Philanthropist*, *Savages*, *Tales from Hollywood*, *Les Liaisons Dangereuses*, *White Chameleon* and *The Talking Cure*. He has translated plays by Ibsen, Molière, von Horváth, Chekhov and Yasmina Reza (including *Art*, *Life × 3*, and *God of Carnage*). His television work includes adaptations of *The History Man* and *Hotel du Lac*. His screenplays include *The Honorary Consul*, *The Good Father*, *Dangerous Liaisons*, *Mary Reilly*, *Total Eclipse*, *The Quiet American*, *Atonement*, *Cheri*, *A Dangerous Method*, *Carrington*, *The Secret Agent* and *Imagining Argentina*, the last three of which he also directed.

CHRISTOPHER HAMPTON

Appomattox

faber and faber

First published in 2012
by Faber and Faber Limited
74–77 Great Russell Street, London WC1B 3DA

Typeset by Country Setting, Kingsdown, Kent CT14 8ES
Printed and bound by CPI Group (UK) Ltd, Croydon, CR0 4YY

A CIP record for this book
is available from the British Library

ISBN 978-0-571-29945-4

2 4 6 8 10 9 7 5 3 1

For Tiana Alexandra-Silliphant

Appomattox was first presented on the McGuire Proscenium Stage of the Guthrie Theater, Minneapolis, on 29 September 2012. The cast, in alphabetical order, was as follows:

Ely S. Parker / Chef M. Cochise Anderson
Ulysses S. Grant / Nicholas Katzenbach
 Mark Benninghofen
Union Guard / Jimmie Lee Jackson / John Lewis Ernest
 Bentley
George Wallace / Confederate Officer Mark Boyett
David Porter / James Bonard Fowler David Anthony
 Brinkley
Cartha Deloach / Edward Alexander Stephen Cartmell
Old Man / Cager Lee Danny Robinson Clark
Abraham Lincoln / Lyndon Baines Johnson
 Harry Groener
Martin Luther King, Jr / T. Morris Chester
 Shawn Hamilton
Viola Jackson Tonia Jackson
Robert E. Lee / Richard Russell Philip Kerr
Mary Custis Lee Karen Landry
John Wilkes Booth / John Rawlins / Lee Harvey Oswald /
 Jack Valenti Michael Milligan
Elizabeth Keckley / Coretta Scott King Greta Oglesby
Howell Cobb / Edgar Ray Killen Richard Ooms
Julia Grant / Viola Liuzzo Angela Pierce
Wilmer McLean / J. Edgar Hoover Brian Reddy
Mary Todd Lincoln / Lady Bird Johnson Sally Wingert

Other parts played by Sha Cage, Brian James, Joe Nathan Thomas and members of the company

Director David Esbjornson
Set Designer Thomas Lynch
Costume Designer Michael Krass
Lighting Designer Jeff Croiter
Sound Designer Scott W. Edwards
Projection Designer Sven Ortel
Dramaturgy Jo Holcomb, Carla Steen
Voice and Dialect Coach D'Arcy Smith
Movement Marcela Lorca

Characters

in order of appearance

1865

John Wilkes Booth
twenty-six

Abraham Lincoln
President of the United States, fifty-six

Frederick Douglass
late forties

Mrs Dorsey
late thirties

Mary Todd Lincoln
Lincoln's wife, forty-five

Ulysses S. Grant
General in Chief of the Armies of the United States,
forty-two

Julia Grant
his wife, thirty-eight

Elizabeth Keckley
modiste to Mrs Lincoln, early forties

General John Rawlins
thirty-four

Robert E. Lee
General in Chief of the Confederate Forces,
fifty-eight

Mary Custis Lee
his wife, fifty-six

Brigadier General Edward Alexander
twenty-nine

General Howell Cobb
fifty

T. Morris Chester
thirty-one

A Confederate Officer

A Union Officer

First Civilian

Second Civilian

Admiral David Porter
fifty-one

An Old Woman

A Man

An Old Man

Wilmer McLean
fifty

Colonel Ely Parker
thirty-seven

A Union Captain

A Union Brigadier

1962

Lee Harvey Oswald
twenty-four

1965

A Disabled Man

A Waitress

A Chef

Jimmie Lee Jackson
twenty-six

Viola Jackson
his mother, late forties

Cager Lee
his grandfather, eighty-two

James Bonard Fowler
thirty-one

A State Trooper

Martin Luther King, Jr
thirty-six

Lyndon Johnson
President of the United States, fifty-six

J. Edgar Hoover
Director of the FBI, seventy

Cartha 'Deke' DeLoach
Hoover's Deputy, forty-four

Nicholas Katzenbach
United States Attorney General, forty-three

Jack Valenti
Special Assistant to the President,
forty-three

Lady Bird Johnson
Johnson's wife, fifty-two

Governor George Wallace
forty-five

John Lewis
twenty-five

First SNCC Man

Second SNCC Man

Senator Richard Russell
sixty-seven

Coretta Scott King
King's wife, thirty-seven

Viola Liuzzo
thirty-nine

2010

James Bonard Fowler
seventy-six

Edgar Ray Killen
mid-eighties

Guests and servants at the White House, a Runner,
a Union Guard, Marines, Residents of Richmond,
Virginia, Couriers, a Medical Officer, an Orderly,
Grant's staff, Lee's staff, a Trooper, Looters,
Customers in Mack's Café, State Troopers,
Members of the Congregation of Zion's Chapel,
Members of the Student Non-Violent Coordinating
Committee, Selma-to-Montgomery Marchers,
a Prison Guard

Note on Casting

The play is designed to encourage cross-casting between the acts. Obviously, this will generally proceed according to the director's taste and requirements, but in the original production at the Guthrie Theater, Minneapolis, the roles were distributed as follows:

Abraham Lincoln / Lyndon Johnson

John Wilkes Booth / Lee Harvey Oswald / John Rawlins / Jack Valenti

Ulysses S. Grant / Nicholas Katzenbach
Robert E. Lee / Richard Russell
Edward Alexander / Cartha DeLoach
Howell Cobb / Edgar Ray Killen
T. Morris Chester / Martin Luther King
Jimmie Lee Jackson / John Lewis
David Porter / James Bonard Fowler
Old Man / Cager Lee
Wilmer Mclean / J. Edgar Hoover
Ely Parker / Chef
Mary Todd Lincoln / Lady Bird Johnson
Julia Grant / Viola Liuzzo
Elizabeth Keckley / Coretta Scott King
Old Woman / Viola Jackson

Certain other roles (e.g. Mary Custis Lee) were not doubled; and all other parts were played by members of the company

Dates and Locations

ACT ONE

1865

ONE	4th March: Capitol, Washington, DC
TWO	4th March: ante-room to the East Room in the White House
THREE	Three weeks later: aboard *The River Queen*, City Point, Virginia
FOUR	Two days later: The Mess, Richmond, Virginia
FIVE	1st April: Dabney's Sawmill, Petersburg, Virginia
SIX	3rd April: House of Representatives, Capitol, Richmond, Virginia
SEVEN	3rd April: The Mess
EIGHT	4th April: Rockett's Landing, Richmond, Virginia
NINE	7th–9th April: various locations in and around Farmville, Virginia
TEN	9th April: Wilmer McLean's house, Appomattox Court House, Virginia
ELEVEN	9th April: Elizabeth Keckley's cabin on *The River Queen*
TWELVE	9th April: Wilmer McLean's house
THIRTEEN	9th April: *The River Queen*, approaching Washington, DC
FOURTEEN	9th April: Wilmer McLean's house

ACT TWO

1962

ONE 11th June: Lee Harvey Oswald's apartment, New Orleans

1965

TWO 18th February: Mack's Café, Marion, Alabama

THREE 3rd March: Zion's Chapel Methodist, Marion, Alabama

FOUR 4th March: the Oval Office in the White House

FIVE 5th March: the Oval Office

SIX 7th March: the Oval Office

SEVEN 11th March: the Oval Office

EIGHT 13th March: the Oval Office

NINE 15th March: the Speaker's chambers, Washington, DC, and Sullivan Jackson's house in Selma, Alabama

TEN A few days later: the Oval Office

ELEVEN 25th March: outside the Capitol, Montgomery, Alabama

TWELVE 26th March: the Oval Office

2010

THIRTEEN December: a state prison in Alabama

APPOMATTOX

Act One
1865

ONE

A face appears, hovering more than fifteen feet above the stage: the handsome, regular features of the twenty-six-year-old John Wilkes Booth. It's 4th March 1865.

Booth

'... Between the acting of a dreadful thing
And the first motion, all the interim is
Like a phantasma or a hideous dream.'

As I stood above him, so close behind his head, on the day of his second inauguration, musing on Brutus, it dawned on me how childishly simple it would be to kill the son of a bitch.

As he speaks, it's as if the sun comes out and lights the cadaverous face of Abraham Lincoln, fifty-six, ten feet directly beneath him, as can clearly be seen in the sole remaining photograph of the event. Lincoln stands at a podium, reading from a single sheet of paper.

Lincoln ... On the occasion corresponding to this four years ago, all thoughts were anxiously directed to an impending civil war. All dreaded it – all sought to avert it. Both parties deprecated war; but one of them would make war rather than let the nation survive; and the other would accept war rather than let it perish. And the war came.

Neither party expected for the war the magnitude or the duration which it has already attained. Each looked for an easier triumph, and a result less fundamental and astounding. Both read the same Bible, and pray to the same God; and each invokes His aid against the other. It may seem strange that any man should dare to ask a just

God's assistance in wringing their bread from the sweat of other men's faces; but let us judge not, that we be not judged. The prayers of both could not be answered – that of neither has been answered fully.

The Almighty has His own purposes. 'Woe unto the world because of offences! For it must needs be that offences come; but woe to that man by whom the offence cometh.' If we shall suppose that American slavery is one of those offences which, in the providence of God, must needs come, but which, having continued through His appointed time, He now wills to remove, and that He gives to both North and South this terrible war, as the woe due to those by whom the offence came, shall we discern therein any departure from those divine attributes which the believers in a living God always ascribe to Him? Fondly do we hope – fervently do we pray – that this mighty scourge of war may speedily pass away. Yet, if God wills that it continue until all the wealth piled by the bondsman's two hundred and fifty years of unrequited toil shall be sunk, and until every drop of blood drawn with the lash shall be paid by another drawn with the sword, as was said three thousand years ago, so still it must be said, 'The judgements of the Lord are true and righteous altogether.'

With malice toward none; with charity for all; with firmness in the right, as God gives us to see the right, let us strive on to finish the work we are in; to bind up the nation's wounds; to care for him who shall have borne the battle, and for his widow, and his orphan – to do all which may achieve and cherish a just and lasting peace among ourselves, and with all nations.

As he turns away, raising his right hand preparatory to taking the oath of office, his image fades, leaving only the face of Booth, who, having listened to the speech with a sardonic curl of the lip, now turns slightly to face forward.

Booth However much he tried to pretty it up with all those fine phrases from the good book, I could tell what it was stood behind his words: it was citizenship for niggers. I was there, let me tell you, I was one of the Honour Guard, when our own General Bobby Lee strung up crazy old John Brown in Charlestown. So you could say I was in at the beginning. Now, by God, I am determined to be in at the end. I am resolved this is the last speech he will ever make.

He smiles wolfishly.

> 'I do love thee so
> That I will shortly send thy soul to heaven.'

I'll put him through.

TWO

That evening. An anteroom to the East Room of the White House, where a post-inaugural reception is being held and from which emanates a stupendous cacophony of conversation and music. Guests criss-cross the room, coming and going, as do a succession of liveried servants carrying trays of food and drink. After a while, the strikingly distinguished figure of Frederick Douglass appears. He's in his late forties, formally dressed, with a mane of hair like a biblical prophet. He's accompanied by an elegant and well-dressed woman, Mrs Dorsey. They pause for a moment to orient themselves, then, as they begin to move off, President Lincoln, in his frock coat and formal necktie, appears in the doorway behind them.

Lincoln Mr Douglass!

Douglass and Mrs Dorsey turn, surprised.

Not leaving already, are you?

Douglass I must deliver Mrs Dorsey back to her husband; they are returning to Philadelphia.

Lincoln I can't let you go without asking you: how did you like my inaugural address?

Douglass Well, I . . .

Lincoln I saw you down there in the crowd; I pointed you out to Vice President Johnson.

Douglass acknowledges this with a courtly nod. Lincoln waits, but finally breaks the silence.

Well? What did you think? I assure you, Douglass, there is no man in the country whose opinion I value more than yours. And I know you will speak your mind.

Douglass takes his time: finally answers.

Douglass Mr Lincoln, that was a sacred effort.

Lincoln seems genuinely relieved.

Lincoln I'm glad you liked it.

Douglass I have not been so stirred since that cold New Year's Day in Boston when we heard your Emancipation Proclamation.

Lincoln I don't believe my speech will be immediately popular: men are not flattered when you draw attention to a difference of purpose between the Almighty and themselves.

Douglass No: it is one for the ages.

Lincoln turns to Mrs Dorsey.

Lincoln I was especially anxious to glean Mr Douglass's opinion; I know he always says exactly what he thinks, he once described me as tardy, hesitating and vacillating.

Mrs Dorsey Never uses one word if he can use three.

Lincoln I was forced to plead guilty to the first two charges; but I did have to draw the line at vacillating.

Douglass I withdrew the epithet, Mr President.

Lincoln So you did, Mr Douglass, most gracefully.

Douglass I regret ever having criticised you, sir.

Lincoln Come now, Mr Douglass, the hurly-burly of robust debate is surely one of the glories of our democracy.

Douglass I will allow that, Mr President.

Lincoln And tell me, Mr Douglass, what would you most like to ensue from the second term we have been fortunate enough to secure? I leave aside the successful conclusion of the war, which my generals assure me is imminent.

Douglass Suffrage, sir. Voting rights for all free men of colour.

Lincoln Well, I have little doubt you will continue to find me hesitating and tardy, but it is my intention to begin gingerly advancing along that path.

Douglass It's a profound satisfaction to me to hear you say that, Mr President. But we've detained you long enough from your guests.

Lincoln No, no, my friend, our opportunities for conversation are so rare, we must make the most of them. Last time we met, I was most impressed with your plan to send scouts to recruit slaves to join our armies.

Douglass That was your idea, Mr President.

Lincoln Was it? I could have sworn it was yours; in any event, it was an excellent initiative.

Douglass I look forward to the prospect of further discussions, when you are more at your leisure.

Lincoln Of course; and I do apologise for the difficulties you experienced when you arrived.

Douglass Please don't trouble yourself, Mr President . . .

Lincoln Oh, but it does trouble me: what did the officers say to you?

Douglass It's of no consequence, sir, I'm sure they thought . . .

Lincoln Please, Mr Douglass, tell me what they said.

Douglass They said their orders were to admit no . . . persons of my colour to the White House.

Lincoln Is that exactly what they said?

Douglass That was their meaning.

Lincoln turns to Mrs Dorsey.

Lincoln An absurd thing to say: this is Mr Douglass's third visit here, at least.

Mrs Dorsey It was nothing we hadn't heard many times before, Mr President.

Lincoln It's a pleasure to make your acquaintance, Mrs Dorsey. I hope perhaps to sample your husband's celebrated cuisine when next I'm in Philadelphia.

Mrs Dorsey It would be an honour, Mr President.

Lincoln shakes her hand and then takes Douglass's hand in both of his.

Lincoln Always happy to see you, Douglass: and I want to tell you, if our plans come to fruition, you need feel under no obligation to vote Republican.

Douglass I can't imagine what circumstances would make me vote any other way, Mr President.

He turns, takes Mrs Dorsey's arm and leaves the room with her. Lincoln watches them go, then, with the slightest trace of reluctance, steels himself to return to the clamour of the East Room. But before he can set off, Mary Todd Lincoln appears, a once-handsome woman of forty-five, wearing a spectacular white silk dress with a bertha of point lace and a lace shawl. She has jasmine and purple violets in her hair and carries an ermine fan with silver spangles.

Mary Lincoln There you are – your guests are asking for you, what are you doing skulking out here?

Lincoln I was just saying goodbye to Mr Douglass, Mother.

Mary Lincoln Mr Frederick Douglass?

Lincoln Yes.

Mary Lincoln Where is he?

Lincoln He just left.

Mary Lincoln But he was the one person I particularly wanted to meet.

Lincoln Oh.

Mary Lincoln Why did you not introduce me to him?

Lincoln I assumed he had been presented. I'm sorry, Mother. It was an oversight. The poor fellow had the greatest difficulty getting in at all.

Mary Lincoln What do you mean?

Lincoln Two policemen at the door told him no Negroes in the White House. He refused to leave. In the end, someone let me know he was down there and I had him brought up.

Mary Lincoln Did he give you their names?

Lincoln Whose names?

Mary Lincoln The policemen.

Lincoln No, why?

Mary Lincoln To have them dismissed.

Lincoln frowns at her.

They must be dismissed. This kind of conduct cannot be tolerated.

Lincoln I suppose they were only doing what they thought was right.

Mary Lincoln It's not good enough.

Lincoln I thought you said our guests were fading away without me. Shall we return?

Mary Lincoln By all means.

She takes his arm. They head back towards the noise and the light.

I shall have this looked into.

THREE

Three weeks later. The saloon of the Presidential steamboat, The River Queen, *which is moored at the docks in City Point, Virginia. President Lincoln is conferring with Ulysses S. Grant, forty-two, General in Chief of the Armies of the United States. Grant has made some considerable effort to look presentable, but, as always, he has somewhat the air of an unmade bed, his buttons not entirely under control and his hair and beard obstinately unruly. He sits, as the President paces.*

Lincoln You're telling me Fort Stedman has fallen? Fort Stedman!

He has spoken with such uncharacteristic intensity that Grant is temporarily taken aback.

I'm sorry, I thought it was only a matter of days, I thought there was to be no more of this kind of thing: and now you tell me Fort Stedman has fallen!

Grant At 5:30 this morning. I ordered an immediate counter-attack, which should by now have succeeded. It's just a little rumpus up the line.

Lincoln I need hardly tell you, the purpose of my re-election was to bring to an end as expeditiously as possible this glut of blood.

Grant With that aim, Mr President, we are putting all our effort into slamming the door on General Lee.

Lincoln Lay that out for me a little, will you, General Grant?

Grant Reason he launched this half-crazy attack this morning was to try to force me to contract my lines, so he can slip through them and join up with General Johnston in the Carolinas.

Lincoln Which if he did?

Grant He could prolong the war another year.

Lincoln You'd better tell me that's not going to happen.

Grant lowers his head briefly. Then he looks up again, his expression steadfast.

Grant It's not going to happen.

Lincoln Because?

Grant I'm sending General Sheridan to attend to the door.

Lincoln You like him, don't you?

Grant Little Phil. He should be here tomorrow.

Lincoln I used to think he was a foot too short to be a general.

Grant I call him my left-hand man. And I'm left-handed. May I smoke, Mr President?

Lincoln By all means. So you think you have the bear by the hind leg?

Grant nods, fishing a cigar stub out of one of his pockets and a match from another, which he strikes. He inhales greedily.

Grant I should also tell you General Wilson is making excellent progress down through Alabama. He should be in Selma within the week to destroy the manufactories there.

Lincoln Selma, good. But that's a long way off. I'm more concerned with bottling General Lee.

Grant It must be said, Mr President, Lee being Lee, I think we should expect at least one more desperate bloody battle. Maybe when Richmond falls.

Lincoln And when will that be?

Grant Next week, I hope.

Lincoln Well, good; but . . . my God, General, can we not avoid this battle? Can you not spare more effusions of blood? We've had so much of it.

Grant says nothing; but his expression clearly signals that the answer is no.

Grant If, as I surmise, the surrender of the rebel armies is imminent, the question arises as to what should be done with them.

Lincoln Yes, this should be the heart of our discussion. And the answer is: we should be generous. I want those men back to their homes, their shops and their farms. As soon as they lay down their arms, they will be guaranteed all their rights as citizens, and need fear no reprisal. Agreed?

Grant Does that apply to all those politicians up in Richmond? I know a lot of people would be happy to see them strung from the nearest lamp post.

Lincoln It's true, I have to be a little more circumspect when it comes to civilians. So let me put it this way: a teetotaller, after a long and tiring journey, was asked if he wouldn't prefer his lemonade rejuvenated with a little brandy. He said, 'I can't see what harm it's going to do, long as nobody tells me about it.' I mean, if you care to issue Mr Jefferson Davis and his crew of traitors a safe passage out of the country, that'll be fine by me, just so long as nobody tells me about it. I make myself clear?

Grant Yes, Mr President.

Lincoln But for the fighting man, General Grant, what I say is, let him up easy. Let 'em all up easy.

Grant Understood.

He scrambles to his feet and stubs out his cigar as Mary Todd Lincoln, this time wearing an elaborate hooped purple dress (second-degree mourning), sweeps into the saloon. She's accompanied by Grant's wife, Julia, thirty-nine, plainly dressed, self-contained and trim; and Elizabeth Keckley, Mrs Lincoln's modiste and confidante, a strikingly good-looking black woman in her early forties. Mrs Lincoln, though she is making an effort to control it, is clearly extremely agitated.

Mary Lincoln Ah, General Grant, the very man! I must congratulate you for at last deciding to relieve General Ord of his command.

Grant But I haven't, ma'am . . .

Mary Lincoln No? I think you should.

Lincoln My dear, I don't believe . . .

Mary Lincoln ignores him completely and continues talking to Grant.

Mary Lincoln General Ord sent an ancient, most uncomfortable carriage, an ambulance I later learned, which would account for its unfortunate odour, to bring your wife and me to the review. We were shaken half to death and naturally arrived late: only to discover Ord had sent *his* wife to ride beside Mr Lincoln at the inspection. How could he suppose the President would wish to be seen next to that wretched woman, with her ridiculous hat? Is that the kind of judgement he exercises in the field? Or perhaps he planned the whole thing?

Julia Oh, no, I don't think that could be the case . . .

Mary Lincoln Do you not? I must say, if you want to reach the White House yourself, you'll need to show a little more discernment.

Julia I have no thought of reaching the White House.

Mary Lincoln Is that so?

Julia I never imagined we would rise to where we are.

Mary Lincoln I tell you, if you can get the White House, you'd better take it. There's plenty to be said for it. It's very nice.

Lincoln I am, in fact, in conference with the General.

Mary Lincoln Oh, are you? Then I won't detain you. I have one very simple question. Did you see that woman alone?

Lincoln Come, Mother, these are matters we should speak of in private.

Mary Lincoln Answer the question! Did you see that woman alone?

Lincoln There were at least a thousand people present.

Mary Lincoln And Mrs General Griffin yesterday? Did you make an assignation with her?

For a moment, Lincoln is at a loss; then, with some dignity, he draws himself up and begins moving towards the door.

Lincoln I am retiring, Mother; would you join me?

Mrs Lincoln turns to Elizabeth Keckley.

Mary Lincoln Come, Lizabeth.

She leaves the room, followed by Elizabeth Keckley. Silence. Grant and Julia look at one another. There's a sense of a great shared understanding between them.

Julia This has gone on for hours.

Grant And it's why I thank God daily for your strength and calm.

Julia How is the President?

Grant Anxious for the bloodletting to stop.

Julia You promised me that that would happen soon.

Grant And so it will; but not just yet.

Julia It's high time.

Grant What put Mrs Lincoln into such a passion?

Julia It was because of her we were late: she was deciding what to wear. I suppose it's fortunate she's in mourning, or the choice could be detaining us still. Then the roads were worse than ever: once we bounced so lively over the corduroy, she hit her head against the roof of the carriage and disarranged her bonnet. At one point, knowing how late she was, she screamed at the driver to stop and let her down, but the mud was too deep and soiled her silk train. They'd delayed the ceremony as long as they could, but by the time we arrived, it was well under way. Poor Mrs Ord in her Robin Hood cap rode over as soon as she saw the carriage, but the damage was done and Mrs Lincoln dressed her down in front of everyone. Now the President will be getting it in the neck.

Grant Do you wonder I prefer to be in the field under canvas? Is Rawlins aboard?

Julia He's out on deck.

Grant Would you send him to me?

> *Julia gives him a gracious smile and leaves the room. Grant digs out another half-smoked cigar and lights it. He moves around the room, coming to rest at a sideboard on which temptingly nestles a cluster of decanters. He looks up as his chief of staff, General John Rawlins, thirty-four, steps into the room, a pale, intense-looking man with a thick, dark beard. He's an old friend of Grant's from their days in Galena, Illinois.*

What news?

Rawlins We took back Fort Stedman.

Grant Thank the Lord.

Rawlins All should be well, unless . . .

Grant Unless what?

Rawlins You never know with Lee.

> *Grant sighs exasperatedly.*

Grant Lee is mortal, Aaron. You always speak of him as if he were some supernatural being who can turn two

back-somersaults in mid-battle and land behind my lines.
I need a drink.

Rawlins No!

Grant Keep your hair on.

Rawlins A goddamn drink is what you do not need!
I must appeal to you. No more responsibility has lain
across the shoulders of an American since Washington
crossed the Delaware. I'd rather see you take a glass of
poison!

Grant For God's sake, Aaron, I know you've picked me
off the sidewalk in Galena a time or two, but all the
same. I only said I needed a drink, I didn't say I was
about to pour myself three fingers of bourbon.

Rawlins I'm sorry, you know how strongly I feel about
this.

Grant shakes his head, then decides to move on.

Grant Fort Stedman . . .

Rawlins Yes. Lee has lost the best part of five thousand
men today.

A low whistle from Grant.

Grant That's a tenth part of his army. What of us?

Rawlins Somewhere above two thousand.

Grant lowers his head, stricken.

FOUR

*A day or two later. The verandah of The Mess, the house
in Richmond, Virginia rented by Robert E. Lee, General
in Chief of the Confederate forces. Lee, a handsome,
impeccably turned out, white-bearded man of fifty-eight,*

17

is talking to his wife, Mary Custis Lee, fifty-six, who sits in the wheelchair to which her rheumatoid arthritis has now largely confined her. In attendance, discreetly hovering at the far end of the verandah, is Lee's aide, Brigadier General Edward P. Alexander, twenty-nine, a tall man with a dark beard, supervisor of the Richmond defences.

Lee To avoid being surrounded, I shall have to abandon our positions here in Richmond, which means the city will be wholly undefended. I don't understand, Molly, why I cannot prevail on you to leave.

Mary Lee We did so last year; turned ourselves into refugees and drifted helplessly around for months on end. I'll never do that again: I'd rather stay in my house and trust to Providence.

Lee As you wish.

Mary Lee As it is, our home in Arlington is overrun with Federal troops. I'm told our own slaves are not even allowed to tend my parents' graves. You said we should show Christian resignation. Very well, then: I will do that by staying where I am.

Lee I'm very much afraid there may be anarchy and looting.

Pause. Mary Lee looks up at him.

Mary Lee So is this the end?

Lee If we can break through Grant's lines and rendezvous with Johnston, we'll be able to regroup and fight on. I see no reason why we can't recruit three hundred thousand slaves.

Mary Lee You know I can't approve of this idea.

Lee I have to use whatever means I may, if I'm to keep our cause alive. And now you must excuse me, my dear, my visitor is approaching. General Alexander, would you be so good as to take Mrs Lee into the house and see her settled? Then return and join us.

Alexander Yes, sir.

Lee I shall come in, Molly, and make my farewells by and by.

Alexander takes hold of Mary Lee's wheelchair and rolls her into the house. As they disappear, Howell Cobb arrives. He's a stout fifty-year-old with an authoritative manner, a former Speaker of the House of Representatives and Secretary of the Treasury. Lee shakes hands with him warily.

Ah, General Cobb. I understand you've been paying a visit to the Congress. What did you find there?

Cobb Rather a shortage of brains, I'm sorry to say.

Lee I've given up expecting much from them. All they seem to be able to do is eat peanuts and chew tobacco, while my army starves.

Cobb Nevertheless, my business with you does concern Congress: I hope you don't mind my taking up your time.

Lee I'm aware you were designated by President Buchanan as his successor; whatever you have to say is certain to be worth my attention. Though I'm sure you'll understand if I ask you to be brief.

Cobb As you know, three weeks ago, the Congress authorised the use of slaves as combat soldiers in the state of Virginia.

Lee Yes.

Cobb And they're not even to be segregated, as is the enemy's practice, but will be fighting shoulder to shoulder with our troops.

Lee Yes.

Cobb Will you not ask them to repeal this bill?

Lee Why do you ask *me* to do this?

Cobb The Congress will not venture to deny you anything you may ask.

Lee But why should I ask *this*?

Cobb Well, because this is the most pernicious bill ever passed by our Congress. It makes a mockery of our Revolution.

Lee If this bill had been passed last year when it was first mooted, after winter training, I could have had twenty more divisions in the field.

Cobb If you can make good soldiers out of slaves, where does that leave our theory of slavery? Do you say it's wrong?

Lee My business is war, not theorising. I don't want to read on the Confederacy's tomb, 'Died of a theory.'

Alexander steps back on to the verandah. Lee turns to him.

Would you make sure Traveller is saddled and bring him round? The General is just leaving.

Alexander Yes, sir.

> *He steps down from the verandah and moves away from the house. Lee turns courteously back to Cobb.*

Lee No doubt you are heading back to Georgia. I was sorry to hear your property had been levelled by Sherman.

Cobb Is it true, then, sir, what is rumoured of you in the newspapers: that you are an emancipationist?

Lee Ah, the newspapers. Have you noticed how they are run by all our best generals? Whenever I find defects in the planning of my battles, as I sometimes do while I am fighting them through, I invariably discover these gentlemen foresaw every mistake, even if, sadly, they forgot to warn me in time.

He smiles frostily at Cobb, who has risen to his feet.

Cobb I fail to understand how a good Southerner could contemplate the use of Negro soldiers. I would sooner recruit from the jails.

Lee Let me try to make my position clear to you, General Cobb. My task is to win the war. Striking romantic poses does not tempt me. The fact that I view slavery as a moral and political evil is neither here nor there. Please don't let me keep you.

Cobb jams his hat on his head and disappears into the night.

FIVE

The early hours of 1 April. Dabney's Sawmill, south of Petersburg, Virginia, which has been commandeered for use as General Grant's HQ. Grant sits at his desk, his pen flying across the paper. A Runner stands waiting nearby and Julia Grant sits, reading a book and occasionally glancing anxiously at her husband, on the other side of the room. Rain is drumming heavily on the roof; this will diminish in intensity and eventually stop in the course of the scene.

Grant finishes writing, blots his dispatch and hands it to the Runner.

Grant To General Sheridan.

Runner Sir.

The Runner takes the dispatch and hurries out into the rain. Grant rubs his eyes.

Julia Can you get some rest, Ulys?

Grant Perhaps.

He takes a cigar off his desk and lights it.

I think, soon, it may be possible to end the matter.

Julia You mean surrender?

Grant No, not yet: Lee has at least one more big fight in him.

Julia Why should he want to fill thousands more unnecessary graves? The futility . . .

Grant I don't know. If the truth be told, his cause must be one of the vilest and least forgivable a people ever fought, yet nobody knows, I suspect, what he thinks about it. No one can penetrate his dignity. All the same, I feel sure he suffers at the ceaseless killing of our countrymen. Thousands yesterday and the day before and no doubt thousands more later today.

He shakes his head.

Julia I can see it eats at you from within.

Grant I never expected to become, what did that newspaper call me, 'the architect of death'.

Julia Who would have thought ten years ago, when you were building Hardscrabble Farm with your own hands . . . ?

Grant And so broke I couldn't afford to buy cabbage seed.

Julia I'll never forget you pawned your watch to buy Christmas presents for the children.

Grant And only five years ago I was a clerk in my brothers' store.

Julia That stench all the time from your father's tannery!

Grant Trying not to drown myself in bourbon. Without the war I'd still be there.

Julia And yet my mother always said one day you would be one of the highest in the land. Her faith never wavered for an instant.

Grant She also believed God made the world in six days. If that Colonel Mattoon hadn't been incapable of controlling his men, I'd probably be the regimental baker. It's all chance.

Julia Not entirely. Strange what Mrs Lincoln said about our getting to the White House.

Grant God forbid! At least I know more or less what I'm doing in the army.

Silence. Grant listens for a moment.

It's stopped raining.

He opens a door and looks out into the night. Julia comes up beside him and takes his hand.

Julia Is that good, Ulys?

Grant Yes. Unless the fog comes up with the dawn.

He turns to smile affectionately at her.

Two nights from now, Weitzel should be riding into Richmond.

SIX

3rd April. The Chamber of the House of Representatives in the Confederate Capitol. The spacious hall is in some disarray – scattered papers, upturned chairs – and sparsely populated: a couple of Civilians in one corner engaged in quiet conversation and a Union Officer in dress uniform and sword in another. The eye, however, is drawn to the Speaker's chair, on a raised dais, where an urbane-looking, elegant thirty-one-year-old black man sits writing, using the desk in front of him. This is T. Morris Chester.

Presently, a paroled Confederate Officer, unarmed and, despite his best efforts, somewhat shabby, enters and begins crossing the room. He glances at the Speaker's chair, does a double take and stops in his tracks, horrified. He takes a moment to regain his composure.

Confederate Hey, nigger!

Chester ignores him completely, carries on writing.

I say, nigger!

Chester finishes writing his sentence and looks up.

Chester Are you addressing me, sir?

Confederate You see any other niggers in here?

Chester I see some other gentlemen. And you.

Confederate Come out of there, you black bastard!

Chester I'm not sure you appreciate your position, sir. Richmond has fallen.

By now, the attention of the others in the room has been caught. They watch, riveted.

Confederate Do you know where you are?

Chester Why, yes, this used to be your Capitol, and I believe this room was known as the Hall of Congress. And I am seated in the Speaker's chair.

Confederate Well, get the hell out of it or I'll knock your brains out! Who do you think you are?

Chester I'm reasonably sure I'm T. Morris Chester, special correspondent of the *Philadelphia Press*.

Confederate You goddamn uppity nigger, come out of there!

Chester So this is the celebrated Southern courtliness.

Confederate Why, you . . .

He takes the steps at a run and grabs hold of Chester's collar. Unperturbed, Chester lays down his pen, rises to his feet and delivers a powerful punch to the Confederate's nose, sending him crashing down the stairs in an ungainly heap. Then he sits down again and takes up his pen. The Confederate, boiling with rage, scrambles to his feet and turns to the Union Officer.

Lend me your sword. I'm going to cut this goddamn nigger's heart out!

Union Officer No, I'm not going to do that. But I tell you what I will do. We'll move some chairs, make a ring and you can fight him fair and square. These gentlemen will join me, I'm sure, to see nobody interferes.

The two Civilians indicate their agreement, and Chester rises to his feet.

I believe I'm going to enjoy this.

The Confederate looks around him for a moment, bested; then, as Chester begins to take off his frock coat, he gives a cry of rage and disgust and hurries out of the hall. Chester laughs and puts his coat back on.

Chester Well, thank you, gentlemen. I hope you don't mind, I felt like exercising my rights as a belligerent.

Union Officer Are you really a newspaperman?

Civilian I didn't know they had . . . coloured correspondents.

Chester As far as I know, they have one.

Second Civilian You mean they let you write stories and everything?

Chester Perhaps you'll allow me to read you part of my article. I'd welcome your comments.

Not waiting for any further encouragement, Chester walks up to the dais, picks a sheet of paper up from the desk and reads.

Seated in the Speaker's chair, so long dedicated to treason, but in the future to be consecrated to loyalty, I hasten to give a rapid sketch of the capturing of Richmond. Brevet Brigadier General Draper's brigade of coloured troops were the first infantry to enter the city. Along the road on which the troops double-quicked, batches of Negroes were gathered together, testifying by unmistakable signs their delight at our coming. General Weitzel and staff passed by at a rapid speed and rode up Main Street amid the hearty congratulations of a very large crowd of coloured persons and poor whites, who were gathered together upon the sidewalks manifesting every demonstration of joy. The highest degree of happiness attainable on earth is now being enjoyed by the coloured people of this city. Nothing can be more amusing than the efforts of some of the most violent rebels to cultivate the friendship of the coloured people, with the hope that the forgiving nature of the race may induce them to forget the wrongs of the past and befriend them. What a wonderful change has come over the spirit of Southern dreams!

He stops reading and looks up. Silence.

Civilian I sure hope you're right, son.

Union Officer Perhaps you'll want to revise that after what just happened.

Chester No, I believe we will all now reap a golden harvest.

SEVEN

That evening. The verandah of The Mess. Mary Lee, still in her wheelchair, sits, industriously knitting socks, of which a small pile grows beside her. From time to time she glances disapprovingly at the armed Union Guard who stands at the other end of the verandah – a black soldier in a Federal uniform. She looks up, apprehensive but defiant, as General Rawlins arrives on the verandah.

Rawlins Mrs Lee?

Mary Lee Why, yes.

Rawlins My name is General Rawlins. General Grant has sent me.

Mary Lee Oh, yes? Why did he not come himself?

Rawlins General Grant is not in Richmond. He is detained by other duties.

Mary Lee I see. And what is your business?

Rawlins General Grant wishes to be reassured of your safety and well being. He wants to know that you and your family have been humanely treated.

Mary Lee Well: I received a comfortable armchair from the President, by which I mean, of course, President Davis, who had the goodness to concern himself with the subject of my arthritis. Other than that I wouldn't say our treatment has been especially humane.

She turns to stare fixedly at the black Guard. Rawlins follows her gaze, but does not, for the moment, grasp its import.

Rawlins I'm sorry to hear that.

Mary Lee points at the Guard.

Mary Lee We felt this, for example, could only be a deliberate insult.

Rawlins frowns at the Guard, still not understanding.

Rawlins Has he been impolite?

Mary Lee No, not in the least. His courtesy is neither here nor there.

Rawlins finally grasps what she means.

Rawlins Oh, of course. I'm so sorry. This must have been a simple oversight. There was certainly no intention to demean you. Allow me to deal with this.

He goes to the Guard and speaks quietly to him. The Guard salutes and exits smartly. Rawlins returns to Mary Lee.

I'll wait with you a while, if I may, Mrs Lee; until some . . . suitable replacement can be found.

Mary Lee You mean, I trust, a white man.

Rawlins Indeed, ma'am. And please accept my sincere apologies. Put it down to the anarchy of war.

Silence.

Mary Lee After such a long campaign, it must have been galling to march in and find you'd gained no more than a few handfuls of ashes.

Rawlins We expected Confederate command to destroy bridges, magazines, ironclads, before evacuating the city.

Mary Lee But not perhaps all the tobacco warehouses and the flour mills.

Rawlins No, perhaps not.

Mary Lee The end is not yet, you know. Richmond is not the Confederacy. And you see how well our boys have understood their orders. Leave not one stone on another if it might benefit the enemy.

Rawlins Only regrettable that most of the inhabitants of the poorhouse near French Garden Hill were not warned in advance of the intention to explode the magazines and were consequently incinerated.

Mary Lee looks up at him, a half-smile on her face.

Mary Lee Yes, put it down to the anarchy of war.

EIGHT

4th April. Rockett's Landing in Richmond, a primitive jetty. Abraham Lincoln, accompanied by Admiral David Porter, fifty-one, and a small honour guard of Marines in short jackets and baggy trousers, has just landed. Already a crowd has formed, all black, the majority freed slaves, who cluster around Lincoln. This causes some alarm among the Marines, who instinctively start to shove the crowd back, but Lincoln raises a hand to restrain them and begins shaking hands with those surrounding him. Admiral Porter looks on anxiously, as the crowd hails the President.

Crowd Hallelujah! / Glory hallelujah! / Bless the Lord! / You come to free your children from bondage!

Porter I don't think we should venture into the city with so small an escort, Mr President.

Lincoln It's as well to be humble.

An Old Woman clings on to his hand.

Old Woman I knowed you soon as I seen you, Father Abraham. Four long years you been in my heart. And now I take your hand.

Lincoln And you're free now, ma'am. Free as air.

Old Woman Now I hold your hand, Father, I *know* I'm free.

Porter Would you let the President through now, please?

Man Don't leave so soon, Master Lincoln. We have been many years in the desert without water. Now here we are looking on the spring of life; and, glory to God, it is mighty pleasant!

Lincoln Yes, thank God we have all lived to see this.

An Old Man with white hair comes pushing out of the crowd and falls to his knees in front of Lincoln.

Old Man God bless you, Father Abraham!

Moved and embarrassed, Lincoln stoops to raise the Old Man to his feet.

Lincoln Don't kneel to me. You mustn't kneel. That isn't right. Kneel to God only and thank Him for your liberty. And you may rest assured that as long as I live, no one shall ever put a shackle on your limbs.

Porter Now release the President, please.

Old Man We means no disrespect. We means love and gratitude.

Spontaneously, the crowd begins singing a hymn.

Crowd
    Oh, all ye people clap your hands
    And with triumphant voices sing;

No force the mighty power withstands
Of God, the universal king.

Lincoln listens, increasingly moved; then he raises a large hand.

Lincoln My friends. As I said, you are free as air. You may cast off the name of slave and trample upon it; it will come to you no more. Liberty is your birthright. God gave it to you and it is a sin that you have been deprived of it for so many years. But now, try to deserve this priceless boon. Let the world see that you merit it. Obey God's commandments and thank Him for giving you your liberty, for to Him you owe all things.

The silence which has fallen lasts for a moment longer; then, wild applause and cheers. Lincoln beams at his audience.

There, now. Let me pass on. I want to see the Capitol. I have but little time to spare.

NINE

7th–9th April. Various locations in and around Farmville, Virginia. These represent the different camps of Grant and Lee, as their armies converge on Appomattox Station, and they play out the endgame. Grant is attended by General Rawlins and Lee by General Alexander. Couriers under flags of truce move between the two camps.

Grant finishes writing something and looks up at Rawlins, who is busy with some paperwork of his own. He senses, however, that Grant has something to say to him and puts down his pen.

Rawlins What is it?

Grant I've just written to Lee.

Rawlins You have?

Grant I suddenly had a great mind to summon him to surrender.

Rawlins Goddamn!

Grant Listen to this: 'General, the results of the last week must convince you of the hopelessness of further resistance on the part of the Army of Northern Virginia in this struggle. I feel that it is so and regard it as my duty to shift from myself the responsibility of any further effusion of blood, by asking of you the surrender of that portion of the CS Army known as the Army of Northern Virginia. Your obedient servant, etc., etc.' Will that serve?

Rawlins Admirably.

Grant Really? I'm surprised, you generally have something or other critical to remark.

Rawlins Not this time.

The focus changes to Lee and Alexander, who is just finishing reading Grant's letter to himself. Lee looks up at him. Candlelight.

Lee Well? What do you say?

Alexander Not yet, sir.

Lee You're right. We haven't yet come to that. We have too many brave men to think of laying down our arms. And our men, unlike theirs, still fight with great spirit.

Alexander No comparison, sir.

Lee Tomorrow morning I shall strike him such a blow . . . I'll get you out of this.

Alexander No one here doubts it.

Lee All the same, I suppose it would only be courteous to reply. Will you take a letter?

He takes back Grant's letter, which he refers to as he dictates to Alexander.

'General, I have received your note of this date. Though not entertaining the opinion you express of the hopelessness of further resistance on the part of the Army of Northern Virginia, I reciprocate your desire to avoid useless effusion of blood and therefore, before considering your proposition, ask the terms you will offer on condition of surrender. Very respectfully' – and so forth. Get that out as quickly as possible.

Back at Grant's HQ, Rawlins stands to one side with Lee's letter in his hand, as Grant is attended by an Orderly, who has prepared a mustard bath for his feet and a Medical Officer, who applies mustard plasters to his wrists and the back of his neck: Grant is suffering from one of his celebrated migraines. Rawlins looks up from the letter.

Rawlins Slippery. Very slippery.

Grant But correct. And at least he answered. I'd better write back before this migraine sinks its claws in and blinds me. Let me dictate it to you.

Rawlins sits at the little field desk, pen poised.

Erm . . . 'Your note of last evening in reply to mine is received. In reply I would say . . .' um . . . 'there is but one condition I would insist upon, namely: that the men and officers surrendered shall be disqualified from taking up arms until properly exchanged. I will meet you at any point agreeable to you for the purpose of arranging definitely the terms upon which the surrender of the Army of Northern Virginia will be received.'

Lee's quarters. Candlelight. Lee takes the letter back from Alexander.

Lee And how would you answer that?

Alexander I would not answer it at all.

Lee Ah, but it must be answered. Let me see.

He reflects for a moment, then begins to dictate.

'General, I received at a late hour your note of today. In mine of yesterday, I did not intend to propose the surrender of the ANV. but to ask the terms of your proposition. To be frank, I do not think the emergency has arisen to call for the surrender of this army, but as the restoration of peace should be the sole object of all, I desired to know whether your proposals would lead to that and I cannot therefore meet you with a view to surrender – but as far as your proposal may tend to the restoration of peace, I shall be pleased to meet you at ten a.m. tomorrow on the old stage road to Richmond, between the picket-lines of the two armies.'

Alexander I thought tomorrow morning . . .

Lee Yes. That's right. Tomorrow morning we break out before dawn. By the time he reads it, we should be well on the way to the Blue Ridge Mountains, where I see no reason we may not hold out for twenty years.

Midnight. Grant is curled up, asleep on the floor under a thin blanket. Rawlins appears, clutching Lee's letter and, none too gently, shakes him awake. Not far off, someone is banging out a patriotic tune on an old piano.

Rawlins How's your headache?

Grant groans and sits up groggily, covering his eyes, as Rawlins lights a candle.

Here's something to make it worse.

Grant reads the letter swiftly, then groans again.

Grant It looks as if the old man means to fight.

Rawlins Goddamn old buzzard! Did not intend to propose surrender? Of course he did!

Grant Please don't shout.

Rawlins Cunning old bastard's trying to get better terms! He's trying to trap you into making a peace treaty. You said nothing about that, you asked him to surrender. He asked your terms. You told him. Now he wants to arrange a peace! Never seen anything so underhanded! It's a positive insult!

Grant Oh, Rawlins, it amounts to the same thing. He's only trying to get let down easy. Why don't I meet him in the morning? We can settle the whole business in an hour.

Rawlins No! He deserves no reply whatever. He don't think the emergency has arisen! That's cool of him, I give him that, but it's a goddamn lie! If he hasn't seen the emergency yet, let's show him one and he'll surrender. He has to surrender! By God, it'll be surrender or nothing!

Grant You got to make some allowances, he's in a very trying position. He has to obey his orders, but it all comes down to exactly the same. Why don't I meet him, I'll get him to surrender.

Rawlins No! You have no right to meet General Lee to arrange peace terms. That's the sole prerogative of the President or the Senate. Your only business is to capture or destroy Lee's army.

Grant I have to answer him something.

Rawlins Leave him to stew in his own juices.

Grant covers his eyes again.

Grant The smallest sound or light is blinding me.

Rawlins You want me to stop that piano?

Grant If you would.

Rawlins What is that tune?

Grant No use asking me. I only know two tunes. One's 'Yankee Doodle' and the other isn't.

Rawlins Get some sleep. I'll shut them up.

Grant I'll send the old man an answer in the morning. I can't do it now, I can't think straight.

Rawlins And you'll give him hell?

Grant Yes, yes.

Dawn is breaking. Alexander rushes in to see Lee.

Alexander Dispatch from General Gordon. He says he's fought his troops to a frazzle and has no chance to break through. He says he's facing a solid wall of blue no less than two miles wide.

For the first time, Lee seems visibly shaken; he lowers his leonine head.

Lee Then there is nothing left for me to do but to go treat with General Grant. I would rather die a thousand deaths.

Alexander What will history say, General?

Lee They will say hard things of us, I know. But I will take all the responsibility.

Alexander I can answer for the artillery. They still have as much fight in them as ever.

Lee No, the trouble is lack of infantry.

He sighs profoundly.

How easily I could be rid of all this! I have only to ride along the line.

Pause.

But it is our duty to live.

Alexander If it were to come to this, my idea was to scatter in the bushes.

Lee What would you gain by that?

Alexander Delay. We would take to the woods and scatter like partridges or rabbits. Two-thirds of us could get away and regroup to fight again. Guerrilla warfare. We could hold out for years.

Lee reflects for a moment: then slowly and deliberately shakes his head.

Lee Suppose I accept your suggestion: our men would have no food and be under no discipline. They would have to plunder and rob merely to procure subsistence. The country would be overrun with lawless bands. How many years might it take to recover? It won't do. You young men can go bushwhacking if you like.

Alexander Of course you're right, sir. Forgive me.

Lee We should write to General Grant.

Grant, on his side of the stage, is surrounded by members of his staff. The Courier arrives and hands him a dispatch. Grant flinches, clearly still suffering from his migraine, takes the document and reads. He pales and clenches his teeth; then, expressionless, he hands the letter to Rawlins. Meanwhile, Lee and Alexander have disappeared.

Grant You'd better read this one aloud, General.

Rawlins 'General, I received your note this morning on the picket-line, whither I had come to meet you to ascertain definitely what terms were embraced in your proposal of yesterday with reference to the surrender of this Army. I now ask for an interview in accordance with the offer contained in your letter of yesterday for that purpose. Very respectfully, your obedient servant, Robert E. Lee, General.'

Stunned silence. Then one of Grant's staff takes off his hat, waves it and calls for three cheers. Three ragged cheers; then everyone breaks down in tears, with the exception of Grant, who eventually speaks, dry as a bone.

Grant How will that do, Rawlins?

Rawlins Oh, I think *that* will do.

Grant Would you believe it, my migraine has entirely vanished.

He takes the letter back from Rawlins and contemplates it for a moment.

Let him choose where he wants to surrender. And we'll get it done today.

TEN

Palm Sunday, 9th April. The large front parlour of the house belonging to Wilmer McLean in the village of Appomattox Court House, somewhat formally and fussily furnished by an owner who is evidently a man of means and is now anxiously following General Alexander around as he supervises the preparation of the room for the imminent formal surrender. This consists in clearing a good deal of the furniture to the fringes of the room and replacing it with two small tables, one wood, one marble-topped, each with its own straight chair. McLean is fifty, rather overweight and eccentrically bearded; he's in a state of neurotic agitation. Sounds of horses arriving, offstage.

McLean I'll tell you something, sir, you'll hardly be able to believe: I used to live in a farmhouse near Manassas and during that first great battle of Bull Run, I was taking dinner with General Beauregard, when a Union cannonball landed in my kitchen. So I brought my family down here to Appomattox Court House, where I was assured we'd be far away from the noise of battle and never troubled again. And now . . .

Alexander Now you'll be able to say: the war started in your backyard and it ended in your front parlour.

McLean Well, yes, so I will, the Lord be praised. There is just one thing, sir . . .

Alexander Yes?

McLean Many of these pieces of furniture are antiques, so they're not merely of sentimental value. I'd be most grateful if you could impress that on your men.

Alexander Please don't concern yourself, Mr McLean. I can assure you even the pieces that are not antiques will become extremely desirable: history is about to be made in this room.

From an inner room steps the resplendent figure of General Lee, wearing a new, perfectly tailored grey dress uniform, offset by a blood-red sash and cummerbund, a Russian leather belt studded with gold and an engraved ornamental sword. He looks every inch the victor. He crosses to Alexander and calmly addresses him.

Lee They tell me he's arrived.

And, on cue, the front door opens and General Grant steps into the house, accompanied by a number of his officers including General Rawlins and his military secretary, Colonel Ely S. Parker, thirty-seven, an

Iroquois, a tall, impressive figure. In total contrast to Lee, Grant is wearing the same dirty boots and mud-splattered uniform as before. His tunic gapes open to reveal the government-issue private's shirt beneath. No spurs, no sword, no side arms. He looks, in the words of a contemporary witness, like 'a fly on a shoulder of beef'. He sees Lee and steps forward to shake hands with him, self-consciously buttoning his tunic as he does so.

Grant General Lee.

Lee General Grant. I am delighted to make your acquaintance, sir.

Grant We have in fact met once before.

Lee We have?

Grant During the Mexican War.

Lee Well, now, somebody once told me you and I had met in Mexico; and I've often tried, these last few months, to recollect your face. Without a glimmer of success, I'm afraid.

Grant Oh, I remember you most particularly. You came over from Headquarters to inspect Garland's brigade, in which I was then serving.

Lee Ah, Mexico.

Grant Beautiful town, was it not, Monterrey? All those pomegranate trees. Of course, the war was quite unjust, as it always is when a stronger nation picks on a weaker.

Lee I leave you to be the judge of that, sir.

Grant But I certainly learned a great deal. Not least from you, sir.

Lee It's most gracious of you to say so, sir, but pleasant as it is to chat with you, I believe we have some business to conduct. I imagine the purpose of our meeting is fully understood.

Grant Indeed it is, sir.

Lee I am here to ascertain upon what terms you would receive the surrender of my army.

Grant The terms are substantially those I proposed in my letter: that's to say, the officers and men who are surrendered are to be paroled and disqualified from taking up arms again until properly exchanged. All arms, ammunition and supplies are to be delivered up as captured property.

Lee Those are about the conditions I expected.

Grant Yes. Of course, I hope this may lead to a general suspension of hostilities.

Lee Yes.

Grant And the means of preventing any further loss of life.

Lee Indeed. May I suggest you commit your terms to writing so that they may be formally acted upon.

Grant Very well.

He turns to Parker.

Would you give me my order book?

Parker brings him the order book – yellow, flimsy pages interspersed with carbon paper and a pen and ink. Grant sits at the marble-topped table. As Parker moves off, Lee speaks discreetly to Grant, out of Parker's earshot.

Lee Is he . . . ah, I mean . . . is he a freed man?

Grant No . . . Oh, I see what you mean . . . No, he's a Seneca Indian and a very gifted engineer.

Lee I see.

He looks around briefly, then seats himself at the wooden table, as Grant, after due reflection, begins to write.

ELEVEN

Elizabeth Keckley's cabin on The River Queen. *She is carefully sewing biassed bands of velvet on to a black watered silk dress for Mrs Lincoln. A moment later, Mary Lincoln surges into the room. Elizabeth rises to her feet, laying the dress reverently across her chair. Mary Lincoln presents with a flourish a large, somewhat grubby, pale kid glove.*

Mary Lincoln There you are, Lizabeth, as I promised you.

Elizabeth Thank you so much, Mrs Lincoln.

She takes the glove, delighted.

Mary Lincoln It's none too clean, I fear, with all those hundreds of dirty hands he was obliged to shake. I can't think what you want with it.

Elizabeth I shall always cherish it, Mrs Lincoln, and preserve it for posterity: the glove Mr Lincoln wore at his second inaugural.

Mary Lincoln The poor man is so worn out: and he has another four years to get through. Still, I suppose it's convenient to have won: if nothing else, it has kept my creditors at bay.

Elizabeth How much do you owe, if you don't mind my asking?

Mary Lincoln Twenty-seven thousand dollars.

Elizabeth That is an important sum.

Mary Lincoln Yes, I am in a very narrow place. There are hundreds of Republicans getting rich off my husband's patronage. Immensely rich. At some point I will make a demand of them. The least they can do is advance me the money.

Elizabeth And Mr Lincoln knows nothing of this?

Mary Lincoln God, no! It would drive him mad. He is so straightforward himself, he is always shocked by the duplicity of others.

She picks up the hem of the dress and begins to inspect it.

Beautiful work, Lizzie.

Elizabeth Thank you kindly, Mrs Lincoln.

Mary Lincoln The President has been suffering some most disturbing dreams of late: I wanted to hear your opinion of them.

Elizabeth Of course, ma'am, I will interpret them as best I may: then when we are back in Washington, we can hold a seance and speak to Master Willie on the other shore. He will know exactly how to read them.

Mary Lincoln In the first dream, he lies on his old bed back home in Springfield. He turns his head towards the mirror and sees not one, but two reflections of his face, one, him as he is, the other, beside it, pale as death.

Elizabeth reflects for a moment.

Elizabeth Could be it means that when the war is won, Mr Lincoln will be able to leave by his grief and turn back to be his rightful self.

Mary Lincoln Yes, I see. But the second is more difficult to gloss in such an optimistic way. He was in the White

House, woken by the sound of quiet weeping. Going downstairs to investigate, he could see no one, but the weeping grew louder. Eventually, he reached the East Room, where he saw a throng of mourners surrounding a long black catafalque. The crowd was too thick for him to cross the threshold, so he asked one of the guards whose body lay upon the catafalque. 'Why, sir, the President,' the man replied, 'struck down by an assassin.'

Elizabeth That could not be, since the President himself was standing witness. I think what he saw was the carcass of the war.

Mary Lincoln Then why so many mourners?

Elizabeth They are the troubles of the coming peace, which he knows, being a wise man, will soon crowd around him.

Mary Lincoln Maybe so.

Elizabeth It's strange, being so close as he is to winning his war, that he should be plagued by these morbid fancies.

Mary Lincoln Yes, he's been dreadful solemn all this week. And there was one more dream.

Elizabeth Tell it.

Mary Lincoln He said he found himself aboard a phantom ship, sailing towards a dark, indefinite shore.

Elizabeth looks down, genuinely troubled.

Elizabeth And did he stand alone?

Mary Lincoln Yes.

Elizabeth tries to conceal her growing fear.

TWELVE

Front parlour of the McLean house, Appomattox Court House.

Grant finishes writing, rises to his feet and hands his order book to Lee. He hovers for a moment, then resumes his seat as Lee, moving with all due deliberation, fetches out a pair of steel-rimmed spectacles, produces a spotless white handkerchief from another pocket, fastidiously cleans his spectacles, breathing on the lenses and wiping them vigorously, settles the spectacles carefully on his nose and begins to read. Everyone watches him, riveted. After a while, he looks up.

Lee I believe you may have omitted a word.

Grant I have?

Lee Yes. 'Officers not to take up arms against the government of the United States until properly . . .' Did you intend to use the word 'exchanged'?

Grant Indeed, I thought I had.

Lee With your permission and if you will provide me with a pencil, I will insert the word.

Grant By all means.

He gestures to Colonel Parker who steps forward and hands Lee a pencil, with which he makes the necessary alteration. Then he resumes reading.

Lee Hm. 'Arms and artillery to be turned over . . . This will not embrace the side arms of the officers, nor their private horses or baggage. This done, each officer and man will be allowed to return to their homes . . .'

He looks up, his expression brightening.

This will have a most happy effect upon my army.

Grant I'm glad to hear it.

Lee And I dare say upon the future history of our country.

Grant It is satisfactory, then?

Lee There is one matter I should like to raise.

Grant Yes?

Lee In my army it is not only officers who own their horses. Cavalrymen and artillerists do as well. Will they be permitted to retain their horses?

Grant Not as the terms are presently drawn up.

Lee No, I can see that's been made clear.

He lowers his head sadly; Grant considers for a moment.

Grant I didn't know private soldiers would own their animals. So . . . it's my belief the last battle of this war has been fought; and since I take it most of the men in the ranks are small farmers who will need to put in a crop to carry themselves and their families through the winter, I will arrange it this way: I won't change the terms as now written, but I will give instructions to my officers to let all those who claim to own a horse or mule take their animals home to work their farms.

Lee Thank you. This will have the best possible effect upon the men. It will do much towards conciliating our people.

Grant takes the order book back from Lee.

Grant Then may I have this copied?

Lee By all means.

Grant summons Parker again and hands him the order book.

Grant I'm going to ask you to make us two fair copies, Colonel. My hand is shaking.

Parker Yes, sir.

He sits at Grant's desk and begins writing. A short silence ensues, broken by Lee.

Lee I have a thousand Federal prisoners, General. I should like to arrange their safe return as soon as possible.

Grant Certainly.

Lee I must confess, I have no rations for them. Nor for my own men, come to that.

Grant Ah. Let me arrange for rations to be sent across the lines at once. For, shall we say, twenty-five thousand men, is that enough?

Lee Oh, plenty, plenty, an abundance, I assure you. And a considerable relief.

Grant I was glad to hear you just now make reference to reconciliation. It seems to me that how we end our war today will still be felt a hundred years from now.

Lee I have no doubt you're right, sir.

THIRTEEN

Evening. The saloon of The River Queen. *The sound of the paddle wheels churning.*

President Lincoln is reading to Mary Lincoln and, off to one side sewing, Elizabeth Keckley.

Lincoln

          'Duncan is in his grave;
After life's fitful fever he sleeps well;
Treason has done his worst: nor steel, nor poison,

47

>   Malice domestic, foreign levy, nothing,
>   Can touch him further.'

Shakespeare understood everything: even the way an assassin may envy the peace and calm of his victim. Let me read it again.

>   'Duncan is in his grave;
>   After life's fitful fever he sleeps well;
>   Treason has done his worst: nor steel, nor poison,
>   Malice domestic, foreign levy, nothing,
>   Can touch him further.'

I'll be happy to get back to Springfield in four years' time.

He puts the book aside.

I wonder how Grant is getting on.

Mary Lincoln That man is a butcher.

Lincoln He's done well enough for us, Mother.

Mary Lincoln He's always lost two men to the enemy's one.

Lincoln I should have given you command of the army.

Mary Lincoln Well, better than that obstinate . . . butcher. I've always thought if you'd worked harder at it, you could have persuaded General Lee to lead our armies, as was your original intention.

Lincoln He declined the offer.

Mary Lincoln Perhaps he could have been worked on and his mind changed.

Lincoln He confessed it was the position he had always coveted, but as soon as Virginia declared for the Secessionists he felt he had no choice. Remember he married into one of Virginia's first families. Mrs Lee would never have allowed him to take up arms against their native state, I think we understand how that goes.

Mary Lincoln What do you mean by that?

Pause, as Lincoln decides to change the subject.

Lincoln We shall be landing any minute. I shall drop you and Tad at the White House and travel on to see Seward. The poor fellow is still recovering from his accident.

Mary Lincoln I don't trust that man. I wish you'd never had anything to do with him.

Lincoln If I listened to you, Mother, I should soon be without a cabinet.

Mary Lincoln Seward has no principles.

Lincoln That is no way to speak of our Secretary of State.

Mary Lincoln If a man is an ambitious hypocrite and a politician to boot, you'll generally find it a safe rule not to trust him.

Lincoln All I know is that the poor man has a broken jaw and a dislocated shoulder.

Mary Lincoln You're a saint, Father. Your trouble is that you're too honest for this world. I heard you say you hoped Jefferson Davis would get clean away.

Lincoln That's not quite what I said.

Mary Lincoln Well, I think he must be hanged. He would certainly have hanged you tomorrow, given the opportunity.

Lincoln Judge not, that ye be not judged.

Sound of explosions from the shore: fireworks, perhaps.

Something seems to be going on in the city.

Mary Lincoln Washington: that city is full of enemies!

Lincoln Enemies! I never want to hear that word again.

There's anger in his voice for the first time and Mary Lincoln says nothing. He turns to Elizabeth.

Are you looking forward to the prospect of peace, Madam Elizabeth?

Elizabeth I surely am, sir.

Lincoln It will mean great changes, great improvements for your people.

Mary Lincoln Will you give them the vote?

Lincoln Those who served in our Army, certainly, no one could justify not granting them full citizenship. And we can perhaps extend that to the literate, men who have reached a certain educational level.

Mary Lincoln What about votes for women?

Lincoln Well, I . . .

Mary Lincoln Or . . .

She indicates Elizabeth.

. . . Negro women?

Lincoln Now let's be reasonable, Mother. One step at a time.

The door opens and a slightly dishevelled Admiral Porter appears.

Porter Sorry to burst in on you, Mr President, but people are calling the news from the dock.

Lincoln What news, Admiral?

Porter Lee has surrendered at Appomattox.

FOURTEEN

Mid-afternoon. The McLean house.

   Colonel Parker has two copies of the surrender. He leaves one on Grant's table and takes the other across to Lee. Both men run their eye over the document and sign, Grant eagerly and Lee with weary reluctance. Then they exchange documents and sign again. Parker steps forward to collect the copies. As he does so, Lee extends a hand to him.

Lee Colonel . . . ?

Parker Parker, sir, Ely Parker.

   He shakes Lee's hand.

Lee Good to see at least one real American is present.

Parker We are all Americans, sir.

Lee Very true.

Grant Although it has to be said that Colonel Parker has yet to be granted citizenship by a grateful nation.

Lee I'm sure that is an oversight which will speedily be rectified.

Parker Thank you, sir.

   He withdraws, the documents in hand. Hiatus. Then Lee turns to Grant.

Lee If you'll excuse me . . .

Grant Yes, of course; and I hope you'll forgive me, sir: my uniform, I mean, my boots. I left camp several days ago without my sword and have not seen my baggage since. But I thought you would rather receive me as I am than be detained.

Lee Of course, sir; I'm much obliged to you for doing it in this way.

He shakes hands with Grant, bows to the others, turns upstage and moves away. Everyone falls away from him and he arrives, back to the audience, way upstage, opens the double doors and steps out on to the porch. A voice from the waiting troops offstage stops him in his tracks.

Voice Are we surrendered?

Lee Boys, you can go home; and if you make as good citizens as you have soldiers, you will do well. I . . . I have done the best I can for you. My heart is too full to say more.

Ragged cheers from offstage. Lee puts on his hat and gauntlets and disappears. It's Grant who finally breaks the silence.

Grant Well, Rawlins? Everything to your satisfaction?

Rawlins This will live in history, sir.

Grant No doubt. Couldn't tell what the old man was thinking, could you? He certainly knows how to keep a lid on it.

Rawlins Forget him. How do you feel?

Grant hesitates before answering.

Grant I can't help it, I feel . . . sad.

He turns and leaves the room, his staff following him. Wilmer McLean moves forward, looking around as if to reclaim his house. His comfortable expression lasts only a moment, though, as he's startled by the arrival of a number of men, mostly Union soldiers, plus some civilians. Before he can think of a way to react, a large man, a Captain, lifts one of the chairs where Grant or Lee sat.

Captain How much for the chair?

McLean It's not for sale. These are all my personal possessions.

Captain I'll give you twenty dollars.

McLean I said, it's not for sale.

Brigadier Forty.

The Brigadier, who has suddenly materialised, has the money in his hand, in gold. McLean, increasingly panicked, shakes his head; but the Brigadier simply throws the money on the floor and seizes the chair. But the Captain is not about to give it up and a vicious tussle ensues, which ends in the chair, a light cane affair, coming apart as they struggle. Meanwhile, shadowy figures in the background are disappearing with every item of furniture in the room from the rugs to the grandfather clock. McLean rushes round like a headless chicken, but when he finally settles on a Trooper, who's making off with a lamp, the Trooper simply produces a pistol, and, as McLean retreats, terrified, the Trooper helps himself to the bag of gold on the floor. A wail of protest from McLean.

McLean This is my house!

No one takes the slightest notice of him; and finally, as the lights begin to go down, he stands alone in a room entirely stripped bare.

ONE

A shabbily furnished apartment in a small house in New Orleans. A young man is stretched out on a battered couch, watching a black-and-white TV, on which John F. Kennedy is in mid-speech. It's 11th June 1962; the twenty-four-year-old is Lee Harvey Oswald. It's clearly a sweltering hot day, as Oswald is wearing no more than a brief pair of bright yellow shorts. Plates of half-eaten food and empty beer cans litter the floor. A large photograph of Fidel Castro, clipped from a magazine, is stuck to the wall with Scotch tape.

Kennedy The heart of the question is whether all Americans are to be afforded equal rights and equal opportunities . . .

Oswald You said a mouthful, rich boy.

Kennedy . . . whether we are going to treat our fellow Americans as we want to be treated. If an American, because his skin is dark, cannot eat lunch in a restaurant open to the public, if he cannot send his children to the best public school available, if he cannot vote for the public officials who represent him, if, in short, he cannot enjoy the full and free life which all of us want, then who among us would be content to have the colour of his skin changed and stand in his place? Who among us would then be content with the counsels of patience and delay?

Oswald shouts out loudly, in Russian.

Oswald Marinenka, bring me a soda!

Kennedy One hundred years of delay have passed since President Lincoln freed the slaves, yet their heirs, their grandsons, are not fully free. They are not yet freed from the bonds of injustice. They are not yet freed from social and economic oppression. And this Nation, for all its hopes and all its boasts, will not be fully free until all its citizens are free.

Oswald forms his forefinger and thumb into a pistol and points it at the screen. Then he puts the forefinger of his other hand inside his cheek and makes a popping sound.

We preach freedom around the world, and we mean it, and we cherish our freedom here at home, but are we to say to the world, and much more importantly to each other, that this is the land of the free, except for the Negroes?

Oswald So: it's you and me, motherfucker.

Kennedy That we have no second-class citizens, except for Negroes? That we have no class or caste system, no ghettoes, no master race, except with respect to Negroes? Now the time has come for this Nation to fulfill its promise.

Oswald shouts out again, this time in English.

Oswald Marina! Chrissakes, where are you?

TWO

18th February 1965. Mack's Café in Marion, Alabama. Late evening. The café is more or less deserted: a Disabled Man sits at one of the plain, unadorned tables eating his fried chicken, his crutches leaning against the wall. There's a Waitress and, looking in from time to time, the Chef/Proprietor in his stained white apron. Small lamps are lit on the tables, plates set out in place settings. A short silence is broken by the murmur, in the distance, of a large crowd. The Disabled Man speaks, addressing no one in particular.

Disabled Man They comin' out of the church.

A moment later a voice rings out, speaking through a bullhorn, slightly distorted.

Voice (*offstage*) This is an unlawful assembly. I said this is an unlawful assembly. You are hereby ordered to disperse. Go back to your homes.

A few seconds pass and then, clearly visible through a light change, all the street lights go out, provoking a redundant remark from the Disabled Man.

Disabled Man They turned out the street lights!

Voice (*offstage*) This is your last warning: disperse and return to your homes.

Suddenly, outside in the square, all hell breaks loose, as the police and the State Troopers wade into the crowd swinging their billy clubs. Screams and thuds. The crowd begins to panic and run. It's obviously chaos out there. The Chef has stepped out of the kitchen.

Chef Jesus, what's happening?

The door bursts open and two people run into the café: Jimmie Lee Jackson, twenty-six, and his mother Viola. They're breathless and scared and evidently known to the Waitress.

Witness Jimmie Lee!

But Jimmie Lee has other concerns.

Jackson Where's Grandpaw?

Viola He was right behind us.

Jackson I'll go find him.

> *He surges out of the door; and returns almost immediately, supporting his grandfather, Cager Lee, who's eighty-two and bleeding freely from a head wound.*

Sit down, Grandpaw.

Cager Lee I'm OK.

> *Jackson pulls some paper napkins from the dispenser on one of the tables and mops blood from Cager Lee's temple. He puts the stained napkins down and is reaching for some more when three State Troopers with billy clubs crash into the café; one of them is James Bonard Fowler, thirty-one. The Troopers' first action is to use their clubs to smash out the lights and break as many of the plates as they can readily access, including the one the Disabled Man is eating from. Cager Lee steps forward.*

All we looking for is the right to vote.

> *One of the Troopers lashes out at Cager Lee, who goes down like a skittle. The Disabled Man grabs his crutches and starts hobbling towards the door, as Viola drops to her knees to tend to Cager.*

Trooper Yeah, go on, git!

> *This to the Disabled Man, whom he propels into the night with a kick, toppling him out of the door. Meanwhile, a Second Trooper brings his billy club down on Viola's head with a sickening crack. Jimmie Lee Jackson grabs hold of him as he raises his billy club again, then staggers as he's struck from behind himself. He turns to fight back, but the club hits him in the face and he goes down. The Trooper drags him up*

57

*and hurls him back against a cigarette machine. As
he's in the process of painfully recovering from this,
Bonard Fowler calmly steps forward, draws his pistol
and shoots him twice in the stomach. Everyone stops
moving for a moment; then Viola screams in horror,
and Jackson, his eyes wide and a hand on his stomach
takes a couple of shaky steps into the middle of the
room. Then one of the Troopers hits him again and he
staggers away, still looking astonished, and out into
the street. Yet another club comes down hard on the
back of his shoulder, and he stumbles away into the
darkness.*

THREE

*3rd March. Zion's Chapel Methodist in Marion. The
chapel is packed to bursting with four hundred people,
with twice as many standing outside in the pouring rain,
which can be heard drumming on the roof. All we can
see, however, is a corner of the front row of pews, where
Cager Lee and Viola Jackson sit, still bandaged, with
some of their relatives. Above them, in the pulpit,
vigorous and authoritative, is the thirty-six-year-old
Martin Luther King, Jr: and above him is a home-made
banner, which reads:* RACISM KILLED OUR BROTHER.
*As he speaks, his words are punctuated by the fervent
responses of the congregation ('Yeah!', 'Speak!', 'Tell it!',
'That's right!', 'Yes, sir!', etc.)*

King . . . Like every self-respecting Negro, Jimmie
Jackson wanted to be free: and I never will forget as I
stood by his bedside a few days ago how radiantly he still
responded, how he mentioned the freedom movement
and how he talked about the faith he still had in his God.

A State Trooper pointed the gun, but he did not act
alone. And we must be concerned not merely about who

murdered Jimmie Lee Jackson, but about the system, the way of life, the philosophy which produced the murderer.

So who did kill Jimmie Lee Jackson?

He was murdered by the brutality of every sheriff who practises lawlessness in the name of the law.

He was murdered by the irresponsibility of every politician from governors on down who has fed his constituents the stale bread of hatred and the spoiled meat of racism.

He was murdered by the timidity of a Federal Government that is willing to spend millions of dollars a day to defend freedom in Vietnam, but cannot protect the rights of its citizens at home.

He was murdered by the indifference of every white minister of the Gospel who has remained behind the safe security of his stained-glass windows.

And he was murdered by the cowardice of every Negro who passively accepts the evils of segregation and stands on the sidelines in the struggle for justice.

At times life is hard, hard as crucible steel. But God still has a way of wringing good out of evil.

Jimmie Lee Jackson is speaking to us from his casket; and he is saying to us that we must substitute courage for caution. His death must prove that unmerited suffering does not go unredeemed. We must not be bitter and we must not harbour ideas of retaliating with violence. We must not lose faith in our white brothers –

'Good night, sweet prince,
And flights of angels sing thee to thy rest!'

He lowers his head and, amidst appreciative murmurs and shouts, steps down from the pulpit and shakes hands with Viola and Cager Lee.

Cager Lee Thank you, Dr King. We sure appreciate everything you been doing for us.

King I'm happy I could say a few words.

Cager Lee Jimmie Lee was a deacon at St James Baptist, right here in Marion.

Viola He was such a good boy.

King You heard our brother James Bevel, where he said we're going to have a march from Selma to Montgomery in memory of Jimmie Lee to demand your right to register to vote?

Cager Lee What time you be marching?

King You don't have to do it, Mr Lee, you concentrate on getting well.

Cager Lee What time? I'm gonna be there.

King On Sunday, Mr Lee. Somebody will bring you there.

He's about to move off, then turns back to the old man.

They tell me you keep trying to register.

Cager Lee They don't open the courthouse but two days a month, they give you a number and call it out so you can't hear it, then they go out to lunch and never come back.

King Yes, I know – and that literacy test? You need a college education to understand the questions, and a Master's to answer them.

Cager Lee It's worse in Lowndes County: they make you guess how many jelly beans in a big old glass jar.

King We calculated that at the current rate of registration, it would take a hundred and three years to register the Negroes in Dallas County.

Cager Lee Fast as that?

60

King You see our ad in the *New York Times* last month? Said there were more Negroes in jail with me than there are on the voting rolls in Selma.

Cager Lee I heard that.

King But I'm telling you, Mr Lee, we're going to bring a voting bill into being, you have my word on it.

Cager Lee Amen to that.

King Now, why don't you walk with me to the cemetery? There's so many crazy people out there, I always figure any walk may be my last; but if you good people are next to me, I won't be thinking about that.

He takes Cager Lee and Viola by the arm and leads them out.

FOUR

4th March. The Oval Office. Lyndon Johnson, fifty-six, a tall, restless, overbearing man, presides over a relatively informal meeting at which early evening drinks have been served. Present are J. Edgar Hoover, now seventy, a fastidiously dressed, lizard-skinned figure, overweight but strangely dainty in his movements; his assistant Cartha 'Deke' DeLoach, forty-four, attentive to the point of obsequiousness; Nicholas Katzenbach, forty-three, the Attorney General; and, to one side, the Special Assistant to the President, Jack Valenti, forty-three.

Hoover I would say, Mr President, that to all intents and purposes, Martin Luther King is a Communist. Am I overstating the case, Deke?

DeLoach Well, no, Director, understating it, if anything. I'd say he's definitely a Communist.

Hoover At the very least, he's an instrument in the hands of subversive forces. Less than two years ago, in this very room, King promised President Kennedy that he would break with Stanley Levison, a known Communist, so-called financier, Jewish.

He pauses impressively.

I can tell you that now, as we speak, King is sitting in the Americana Hotel in New York, Room . . .

He snaps his fingers impatiently.

DeLoach 4323.

Hoover . . . Room 4323, being briefed by Levison.

Johnson Is that so? Edgar, you're just as sharp as ever you were in the thirty years I've been privileged to know you.

Hoover Well, thank you, Mr President.

Johnson Jack, go ahead and freshen Mr Hoover's drink, will you?

Valenti leaps to his feet, but Hoover waves him aside.

Hoover I always say you make the best mint julep in Washington, bar none, but I have to be going in a minute.

Johnson You do?

Hoover As long as you're going to be seeing King tomorrow, I thought I should give you a little more background on him.

Johnson You don't like him very much, do you, Edgar?

Hoover I have nothing against him personally, Mr President. He's just a hypocritical degenerate. And *Time* magazine made him Man of the Year! They must have had to dig down to the bottom of the garbage can for that one. And then, if that doesn't take everything, they give him the Nobel Prize! That fraud, that cheap, opportunistic burrhead!

Johnson Degenerate?

Hoover We have him on tape, shouting out . . . you tell him, Deke.

DeLoach He's shouting out: 'I'm fucking for God!' Right here in Washington, in the Willard Hotel.

Johnson Glory be.

DeLoach And he's doing it in front of eight or ten guys standing round watching, all of them buck naked.

Hoover All right, Deke, we get the picture.

Johnson You sure about this?

Hoover Nobel Prize for tomcatting, that's the only Nobel Prize he should ever get.

Katzenbach Plenty of people feel the same as you do, Mr Hoover. Or worse. There were several death threats when he went down to Selma earlier this week, we had to warn him.

Hoover You warned him?

Katzenbach Well, yes.

Hoover If I may take the liberty, Mr Attorney General, I'm not sure that was such a smart idea.

Katzenbach Oh? Why not?

Hoover See, we get to process so many of those things at the Bureau, most all of them from crazies, that we have to make a judgement which ones to pass along. And with someone like King, who's a self-publicist, who chooses to put himself in harm's way, we have a policy not to indulge him with information he's probably just going to look to exploit.

Johnson Well, now, Edgar, when you get in one of these threats, I'm sure you set your people to watch out for him, even if he doesn't know it's happening.

Hoover says nothing, seems to be formulating some response.

I think you should.

Hoover Of course, Mr President.

Johnson How's Clyde doing?

Hoover He's down in La Jolla, Mr President, working on something.

Johnson His tan, that'd be my guess.

Amid general laughter, Hoover, a strained smile on his face, rises to his feet, which causes DeLoach to spring up beside him.

Always wonderful to see you, Edgar.

Hoover What a pleasure, Mr President.

Johnson Jack'll walk you down to your limousine.

Valenti's already on his feet. Johnson nods to DeLoach.

Deke.

DeLoach A great honour to visit with you, sir.

Johnson You take care now.

Valenti escorts them out. Johnson clinks some ice cubes into his glass and pours himself a large Cutty Sark. Then he looks at Katzenbach, shaking his head.

How d'you like that queer old bastard? Isn't he a piece of work?

Katzenbach Certainly is.

Johnson Ain't easy to get him out the door, is it?

Katzenbach I always try to meet in his office. Otherwise I can never get rid of him.

Johnson Lucky for him he's got everybody's balls in a vice. And that Deke DeLoach!

Katzenbach Yes.

Johnson He'd kiss my ass in Macy's window and say it smelled like a rose.

He takes a swig of scotch and his expression changes to complete seriousness.

Nick, have I ever asked you to tap anybody's line?

Katzenbach No, Mr President.

Johnson Don't you have to authorise every wiretap?

Katzenbach Every one made by the FBI. Not the other agencies, Defense or the IRS, though I think it would be a good idea if I did . . .

Johnson Well, I want this brought down to an irreducible minimum. And only in the gravest cases. I want you to authorise them, and then, by God, I want to know about them. I'm a red-hot one-million-two-per-cent civil liberties man and I'm against wiretapping, period. So get up the strongest letter you can and tell all the agencies no one is to be tapped, except by signature of the Attorney General.

Katzenbach A letter to all the agencies?

Johnson Yeah. For me to sign.

Katzenbach All right, Mr President.

Johnson That's how Hoover got the whammy on our friend King, right?

Katzenbach I imagine so.

Johnson Well, who authorised that wiretap?

Katzenbach Uh, that would have been my predecessor.

Johnson Bobby. I might have known. What the hell was he thinking?

Katzenbach I guess it was to do with Levison, you know, King's Communist associates.

Johnson Well, I don't want to know about it.

He thinks for a moment, head nodding.

See, that's why nobody can ever fire that old cocksucker. He has the whammy on everybody. All the same, I'm not sure I don't prefer to have him inside the tent pissing out.

He takes another swig of whisky, chuckles, shakes his head.

'I'm fucking for God'!

FIVE

5th March. The Oval Office again. This time President Johnson is alone with Martin Luther King at the far end of the office, King on the sofa, and Johnson at right angles to him, in his oversized rocking chair, so positioned that the President can loom over and dominate his interlocutor. There's tea on the table, but King, mesmerised, never touches his.

Johnson You know, Martin, my cook, Zephyr Wright, she's been working for us for many years, she's a college graduate – when Miz Johnson and I would fly down to Texas, she and her husband would drive my official car, that's the Cadillac limousine of the Vice President of the

United States, all the way down there, took 'em three days. They'd have to buy food from grocery stores in coloured areas on the edge of town and eat it in the car with plastic spoons. And when they had to go to the bathroom, why, they'd have to pull off on a side road and Zephyr Wright, the cook of the Vice President of the United States, would have to squat down in the road to pee. And that's not right, Martin. It's just wrong.

King I know, Mr President.

Johnson I know you know, I just wanted to try to convey to you how strongly I felt about getting that Civil Rights Bill passed last year, how important it was to me. All the time I was Vice President, I was pushing for it hard as I could, but you know, a Vice President is like a stuck pig in a screwing match. President Kennedy, now I know he sincerely wanted that bill to go through, but he was a little green around the edges, he didn't know how down and dirty you have to get to shift those old walruses in the House and the Senate. I could see we were going to have to get cloture in the Senate, which is about as easy as killing a bull with a set of false teeth – you got to line those ducks up one by one and bribe 'em and pamper 'em and lick their ass and get 'em so they're all ready to shit at the same time when the bell goes. And we did it, we got cloture, thanks to your help, you and your people talking to all those half-dead Republican senators.

King You'd have had a more difficult task with your Southern Democrats.

Johnson You never spoke a truer word: most of them think Judas Iscariot's a good old boy next to me. See, the thing is, Doctor, at the election, I had me a majority of around sixteen million and my guess is we're going to lose that majority at the rate of about a million a month: which gives us just over a year to bring in my education

bills and the War on Poverty Bill and the Medicare Bill –
and, of course, what you're focused on right now, the
Voting Rights Bill. We got to get all them passed before
the vicious forces can concentrate and form a coalition to
block us.

King Yes, I understand, Mr President, but I hope that
doesn't mean voting rights goes back down to the end of
the line.

Johnson Well, the Attorney General's been pushing me
for delay, you know – there's new laws to draft and he
thinks maybe another bill for the nigras so soon after
the Civil Rights Bill may be a problem; but at least I
persuaded him legislation is a far better option than
constitutional reform. I mean, I said to him, we have the
Fifteenth Amendment already, and who the hell ever paid
the least little bit of attention to that? We have to have it
in law.

King I couldn't agree more, Mr President, and I'm so
happy to hear you say this, just not so happy to have to
tell my people they'll have to wait. I don't have to remind
you, sir, that the only states you didn't carry in the South
are the ones where less than forty per cent of the Negroes
are registered to vote. And we feel the thing that'll really
make the new South is going to be the coalition of the
Negro vote and the moderate white vote.

Johnson You're exactly right. And make no mistake, I'm
for voting and we're going to get voting. It's going to go
through like a dose of salts through a widow woman.
Just maybe not this year. But we're working on it all the
time. We've already got Everett Dirksen and a lot of his
Republicans on board.

King Well, that is very good to know.

Johnson So what I want to ask you, Martin, is – do you
really have to go ahead with this march?

King I think the planning may be too far advanced to do anything about it now. It's the day after tomorrow. We did feel, in the face of official silence, we needed to protest the death of this innocent boy.

Johnson You mean Jamey . . . uh?

King Jimmie Lee Jackson.

Johnson Well, that's a shame. I mean it's a shame what happened to Mr Jackson, but it's also a shame to risk provoking, you know, more violence . . .

Silence. Johnson's expression has darkened; but King decides to speak up and say what's on his mind.

King There's one other point I wanted to mention to you. I made a statement on Tuesday concerning the Vietnam situation.

Johnson I saw that, yes. It distressed me.

King It was in no way an attempt to criticise your policies. I know very well the terrible burdens you have to carry, your awesome responsibilities. But I was asked about it – and you know non-violence is the fundamental cornerstone of our beliefs, so I . . . it's like when I'm questioned about South Africa, I can't help but speak out about the treatment of the African population.

Johnson Not everyone's happy about that either, you know, South Africa being one of our strongest allies in the struggle against Communism.

King I'm aware of that, but . . .

Johnson Listen, Doctor, I know you have a right, not only that, you have a duty as a minister and a leader of millions of people to give them a sense of direction, and I respect that. But I can't pull down the flag and come running home bare-ass with my tail between my legs.

I don't deny it's a pretty tough problem, you know, I've had over two hundred and fifty boys killed out there and I know it could easily get a lot worse. I pray every night for judgement to do the right thing.

King I do appreciate your position.

Johnson Well, thank you. Thank you so much.

King God bless you.

Johnson has surged to his feet, extending a hand. There's not much warmth in his expression.

SIX

7th March. The Oval Office is in darkness, it's 9 p.m. Now Jack Valenti leads the way in, switching on the lights, followed by President Johnson, who goes to sit behind his huge desk.

Johnson I hate to drag you away in the middle of your dessert, Jack. Terrible thing to do to a man.

Valenti Oh, that's all right, Mr President.

Johnson Although I think the special assistants to President Kennedy, they had it harder. For example, when he met a woman, lotta times he couldn't remember if he'd fucked her or just made her husband a ambassador.

Valenti Or both.

Johnson That's right. And then there was all the injections he had to have for his condition and the fancy footwork smuggling all those dames in and out of the place and remembering the names of all the nephews and nieces and what-all. Compared to that, looking after me's as easy as a pig eating a daisy.

Valenti I'm not complaining.

The telephone rings on Johnson's desk.

Johnson What time is it, Jack?

Valenti 9:03.

Johnson picks up the phone and listens.

Johnson Yeah . . . Right . . . Everything go off OK? . . .
No casualties? . . . Uh-huh . . . uh-huh . . . What do you
mean, turn on the TV? . . . Oh . . . Oh, I see . . . ABC? . . .
OK.

*He puts the phone down; then, from a console on his
desk, he activates a bank of three huge televisions,
each showing one of the networks, and makes an
adjustment so that he gets the sound from the ABC
network. ABC has broken into its evening movie to
show the day's pictures from Selma: on what was to
become known as 'Bloody Sunday'. Here, by and on
the Edmund Pettus Bridge, State Troopers are firing
tear gas into what had been an orderly crowd; and
then, in their gas masks, many of them on horseback,
are charging the panicking marchers and attacking
them unrestrainedly with billy clubs or lengths of
rubber hose laced with spikes. It's like a scene on a
battlefield. Johnson and Valenti watch for a while,
transfixed.*

Oh, my good God.

He shakes his head, appalled.

It's that fucking Wallace.

Valenti He said he was going to take whatever steps
necessary to prevent the march.

Johnson Jesus.

They keep watching. Presently Lady Bird Johnson steps into the room in her dinner gown. She's a small, immediately sympathetic woman of fifty-two, full of genuine concern, younger-looking than her age.

Lady Bird I thought you boys might like some coffee or a piece of pie . . .

Johnson raises a meaty hand to silence her.

Johnson Look at this, Bird.

She joins them, watching the unfolding events with them for a time.

Lady Bird Is this Alabama? It's terrible.

They watch some more.

Is this why you came over?

Johnson No. No. I came over because I just sent two Marine battalions into Vietnam. They landed at Red Beach 2 in Da Nang at 9:03. The first land combat troops.

She's looking at him, wide-eyed.

Well, what the hell else am I going to do? I couldn't finish it with what I had.

As the television pictures continue, Lady Bird goes over to him and takes his big hand.

I know every mother in the country is going to say uh-oh, this is it.

Lady Bird nods in agreement and looks up at Johnson with an expression of genuine anxiety, which he seems to interpret as reproach.

Shoot, Bird, anyone who can pour piss out of a boot knows I'm doing the right thing in Vietnam.

SEVEN

11th March. Again, the Oval Office is in darkness. This time it's President Johnson who leads the way, switching on the lights, followed by Lady Bird Johnson and Katzenbach. Sounds of an orchestra from below, where the Congressional reception is still in progress; also, faintly, from out on Pennsylvania Avenue, the sound of Civil Rights protesters, chanting: 'LBJ, just you wait, see what happens in sixty-eight!'

Johnson What did that goddamn little pipsqueak from Mississippi say to you, Nick?

Katzenbach He asked me why I was siding with Communist agitators and helping them trample on the rights of the South.

Johnson Asshole. He came out for Goldwater.

Katzenbach They say he's planning to run for Governor.

Johnson He's just about pin-headed enough to win.

He turns to his wife.

OK, Bird, let me just run you through this thing. On Tuesday, King led his people across the bridge again, but when he was challenged, he just said a little prayer and led them right back into Selma. We sent Governor Collins down to oversee those crazy troopers and everything passed off peaceable, he did a good job. So fine. But then in the evening, these three Unitarian ministers from Boston go down to get a little soul food; then afterwards, they're full of sweet potato pie, they take a wrong turn and stray into KKK-country and run into these crackers who call them white niggers, until one of them lets fly with a baseball bat and splits the Reverend Reeb's skull.

Poor bastard struggled a couple days, but they just now switched off the life-support system . . .

One of the phones rings. Johnson lifts the receiver, listens for a moment and hands it to Lady Bird.

Lady Bird Mrs Reeb? . . . May I call you Marie? The President and I just wanted to express how much we feel for you at this terrible time . . . Yes . . . Your husband was a brave man and he gave his life for a wonderful cause, I know that can't be very much of a consolation right now, but I do believe that in years to come you and your children will be able to appreciate that a little more . . .

Johnson extends a hand in her direction.

The President would like to say a few words to you, Marie, please know you really do have my very deepest sympathy . . . Yes . . . Here's the President now.

She hands Johnson the phone.

Johnson Miz Reeb? I just wanted to be able to say to you in person how grieved we are, Miz Johnson and I, and to pay a little tribute to your husband's sacrifice, his supreme sacrifice, really . . . Oh, well now, that's nothing, Miz Reeb, that was Miz Johnson took charge of that, yellow roses are like her trademark . . . Yes, and I want you to know, my plane is available again anytime, when you're ready to take your husband back to Boston . . . Well, bless you, Miz Reeb, you'll be in our prayers, and we're going to do everything in our power to bring those people to justice for you and your children . . . Yes, so be brave and you take care now.

While he's been speaking, Katzenbach has lit a cigarette. Now, as he hangs up the phone, Johnson turns to him.

I could sure use one of your cigarettes, Nick.

Katzenbach Of course, Mr President.

Lady Bird Then I'm going to have to take one as well.

As Katzenbach stands, frowning, his packet of cigarettes extended, Johnson and Lady Bird eyeball one another, in what is obviously a familiar confrontation. Finally, Johnson sighs and drops the hand that was reaching for the cigarette.

Johnson OK, Bird, you win.

Lady Bird Jim and Willis are coming for the weekend, you don't want to have to tell them you've started smoking again.

Johnson You know the first thing I'm going to do, Nick, when I leave the White House? I'm going to light that cigarette, that's what I'm going to do. But if I do it now, Lady Bird's going to have those goddamn physicians all over me like a rash.

Lady Bird You like Jim and Willis.

Johnson Did I say I didn't?

He sighs again and lowers his head.

Same goes for having a drink, huh?

Lady Bird I'll fix you a Fresca.

Johnson Gee, thanks.

She ducks offstage (a tap supplying low-calorie Fresca had been installed in the corridor just outside the Oval Office). In her absence, Johnson turns to Katzenbach, shrugs his shoulders and rolls his eyes.

Mighty smooth operation, uh, getting all those kids out of the White House before the Congressmen arrived?

Katzenbach You managed it much better than we did over at Justice.

Lady Bird has returned with a glass of iced Fresca and a plate of peanut brittle, which she puts down on the corner of the desk.

Lady Bird Are you talking about those demonstrators? Lyndon wouldn't even let me go take a peek at them.

Johnson That's 'cause you'd have wound up inviting them all to brunch.

Lady Bird Has there ever been a sit-in in the White House before?

Johnson I don't think so. Strange days. I keep expecting to run into Lincoln's ghost.

He breaks off a chunk of peanut brittle and pops it into his mouth.

You mind going back down, darlin', and looking after our guests? I need to spend a few minutes with Nick, I'll be right down.

Lady Bird Yes, of course. Nick.

She takes her leave as Katzenbach mumbles an awkward farewell. Silence, except for the crunch of the brittle. Katzenbach blurts out what's on his mind.

Katzenbach I'm so sorry I stopped you making a statement about Sunday's march. I thought we needed to . . .

Johnson Forget it.

Katzenbach No, you were absolutely right, it would have been much . . .

Johnson I said, forget it.

By now, he's round behind his desk, from which he produces a bottle of Cutty Sark. He pours a generous measure into his Fresca.

Drink?

Katzenbach No, thank you.

Johnson Take some brittle, it's great.

Katzenbach snaps himself off a tiny corner of peanut brittle, which he nibbles reluctantly.

Any arrests been made?

Katzenbach Two State Troopers on Sunday. I managed to keep it out of the papers.

Johnson You did? Why?

Katzenbach They beat up an FBI agent who was taking photographs. I knew it wouldn't look good, with all those injured Negroes and the only people we arrest was for attacking a Bureau agent.

Johnson Right. Well, shouldn't we arrest some more?

Katzenbach We may, I'm looking into it.

Johnson What about the crackers who killed the Reverend?

Katzenbach The public safety director in Selma says they'll be charged tonight with first-degree murder. Only problem is, we'll never get a conviction.

Johnson Yeah.

He takes a swig of his drink, ruminates a while.

I guess King handled himself pretty well on Tuesday.

Katzenbach He was in a really tight corner. On the one hand, he's never defied a Federal Court order before, because he knows he can't afford to lose Federal support; on the other hand, if he'd cancelled the march, he's already having a lot of trouble from his left-wingers, he couldn't have let himself lose that much face. So he started the march, gambled the judge wouldn't find him in contempt and then turned around without even knowing, they tell me, if anyone was going to follow him back into Selma.

Johnson And the judge let him off this morning.

Katzenbach That's right.

Johnson And he's going to give permission for the march to go ahead?

Katzenbach Yes, I think so, under certain conditions. I talked to him. So King's played his cards right.

Johnson Yeah. Wish I liked him better.

Katzenbach Well . . .

Johnson When's this march liable to be?

Katzenbach I don't know, a week, ten days . . .

Johnson We're going to have to plan things out real carefully. Because this is going to be the biggest story since de Gaulle farted.

Katzenbach Yes.

Johnson We're going to have to get that runty little bastard Wallace over here. Do you know him?

Katzenbach I had to go to Tuscaloosa and serve him with President Kennedy's proclamation, when he tried to prevent those two black students registering at the University of Alabama. So, yes, I met him. But I don't think anybody really knows him.

Johnson Way I hear it, he's got more twists than a bagful of rattlesnakes. You know what he said when he lost to the KKK's candidate in the '58 election? He said, 'No son of a bitch is ever going to outnigger me again.'

He moves over to the window and looks out for a moment, listening to the distant chanting.

I say those kids are violating my civil rights, what do you think?

Katzenbach Hard to make it stick.

Johnson What's the status of my message to Congress?

Katzenbach I have a draft, but I need to do some more work on it. It doesn't really sing yet.

Johnson Any chance Ev Dirksen will pull out on us?

Katzenbach No, sir, he still wants to be joint sponsor of the bill.

Johnson All the same, I'm going to have to hit it out of the park on Monday. Maybe we should get Dick Goodwin in to help write it.

Katzenbach Whatever you say, Mr President, but maybe take a look at my effort before you decide.

Jonson Sure, Nick, of course. But I have a feeling we're going to need a writer. Congress is a dangerous animal.

EIGHT

13th March. Johnson sits behind his big desk in the Oval Office. He leans forward and presses a button, and a secretary's voice comes on the intercom.

Voice Yes, Mr President?

Johnson Is Governor Wallace in the Cabinet Room?

Voice Yes, Mr President.

Johnson Just stall him in there for five minutes, will you, give him a picture-book or something; and send me in the Attorney General.

Voice Yes, Mr President.

Johnson rises swiftly to his feet and moves to open a concealed door, revealing a smallish bathroom. He unbuckles his belt, lowers his pants and sits on the lavatory. Presently, Katzenbach steps into the empty room, briefcase in hand. He looks around, puzzled, not, for the moment, taking in the open bathroom door.

Johnson That you, Nick?

Katzenbach Uh, yes, Mr President.

Johnson I'm taking a dump.

Katzenbach Oh.

Johnson Come in, come in.

Tentatively, as if walking across coals, Katzenbach puts down his briefcase and ventures into the doorway of the bathroom.

Come right in, you don't have to stand there in the doorway like you were the Avon lady.

Katzenbach tiptoes a couple of feet into the room.

Now, do you have some paper?

Katzenbach grapples with a wild surmise.

Katzenbach Paper?

Johnson To make some notes.

Katzenbach Oh! No. I'll get some.

He steps back into the Oval Office, finds a shorthand pad and reluctantly returns.

Johnson Wallace: what should I ask him to do?

Katzenbach Well . . . what do you want him to do?

Johnson Write me some demands I can make.

Katzenbach Demands?

Johnson Yeah, make a list, any six things, six demands, number them, make them as outrageous as you like.

Katzenbach Ah, yes, sir.

For a moment, there's silence, as Katzenbach leans back against the wall, scribbling furiously and Johnson completes his business, finally rising to his feet, his pants, however, still around his ankles.

Johnson Don't mean to interrupt you, Nick, but I got a question for you.

Katzenbach Yes, Mr President?

Johnson Come here, will you?

Gingerly, Katzenbach approaches. Johnson half turns, pointing at one of his buttocks with a long finger.

Is this a boil on my ass?

Katzenbach Um. . .

Johnson I can't see it from up here.

Appalled, Katzenbach leans forward to inspect the offending item. Then he straightens up.

Katzenbach Looks very like a boil, Mr President.

Johnson I thought so. That's Governor Wallace for you: nothing but a boil on my ass.

He flushes, pulls up his pants, buckles his belt and leads Katzenbach, who's still frantically writing, back into the Oval Office, pushing the bathroom door shut behind him. Then he crosses to the desk and presses a button on the intercom.

Voice Yes, Mr President?

Johnson Send Governor Wallace in, will you?

Voice Yes, Mr President.

Johnson turns to Katzenbach.

Johnson Are you done?

Katzenbach Almost.

Johnson holds out a hand and Katzenbach finishes writing, tears off the sheet of paper and hands it to Johnson , who just has time to glance at it, before the door opens and Governor George Wallace is shown in. Johnson thrusts the piece of paper into his pocket and advances with hand extended to greet Wallace, a shifty little man of forty-five with greasy hair. He looks up at Johnson, who looms over him; he takes his hand with some reluctance, his expression more than a little alarmed.

Johnson Well, it's just wonderful of you to come and visit with us, Governor. This is Nick Katzenbach, my Attorney General. But, of course, you met him in Tuscaloosa, didn't you, when he came with the National Guard to move you out of that schoolhouse door!

Wallace and Katzenbach shake hands; Wallace's expression is thunderous.

And how is Lurleen? My, what a beautiful woman! And your four lovely little kids?

Wallace All very well, Mr President.

Johnson Of course you know Lady Bird's people were from Alabama, she spent every summer in Autauga County, all her childhood till she was a grown woman, talks about it all the time.

Wallace I didn't know.

Johnson Well, now, Governor, did you know you have something in common with Dr Martin Luther King?

Wallace I do?

Johnson You're the only two people ever asked to come see me and told the Press you were coming before I even had time to spit out the invitation.

Wallace Oh, but I thought . . .

Johnson It's all right, Governor, I'm kidding you, it's just my way. Now come over here and sit down, so we can get down to business.

He puts his arm round Wallace and leads him over to the corner of the low sofa where he sat King. Then he sits in his rocking chair, towering over Wallace. Katzenbach chooses a chair on the other side of the table, facing Wallace. Johnson makes a lavish gesture.

You got to try some brittle.

Wallace gives a pinched smile, hoping to avoid the instruction: however, presently, under Johnson's merciless gaze, he feels obliged to take a slab of peanut brittle and put it in his mouth. This means that for the first minute or so of the conversation, his mouth is full of this evidently repulsive and almost unmanageable substance. He's further disconcerted by Johnson's undeviating stare.

Well, now, Governor: what was it you wanted to see me about?

Wallace Mr President, the streets of Selma and Montgomery are crawling with Communists and anarchists, trained in New York and Moscow; and this judge, if I know him, and I do, this irresponsible judge is going to give this riff-raff official permission to make even more trouble. That's not the way to deal with street

83

revolutionaries, which is what we have here. They'll never be satisfied. First they want the front seat on the bus; then they want to take over the public schools; then it's voting rights; finally, they want redistribution of wealth. And they just . . . inflame people, the language they use and the noise they make.

Johnson I know about that: the screaming and hollering those goddamn nigras let out every night on Pennsylvania Avenue is keeping my daughters awake.

Wallace I knew you'd understand, Mr President.

Johnson So what do you want me to do?

Wallace We have very limited amounts of state policemen . . .

Johnson You want me to send in the National Guard?

Wallace Well, yes, that would certainly . . .

Johnson Wait a minute, Governor, whoa there: it's your ox that's in the ditch, shouldn't you be getting him out yourself? Shouldn't you be calling out your Guard?

Wallace I hate to do that, sir. And of course every time I call out the Guard, you-all go and federalise them.

Johnson We do whatever we can to avoid brutality, Governor. I know you hate brutality as much as I do.

Wallace They didn't start all that ruckus, Mr President, it was the outside agitators and the beatniks, it was pure provocation . . .

Johnson You got those photographs, Nick?

Katzenbach opens his briefcase and slides a folder across the table to Wallace, who reluctantly opens it and starts looking at a sheaf of large black-and-white photographs.

Wallace These are . . . isolated incidents.

Johnson It's what happened on Sunday, George, women and children attacked and hospitalised. The whole world saw it on the TV. I think you have to admit there was brutality.

Wallace Well . . .

Johnson The kind of brutality that does us no good at all at home or abroad.

Wallace I suppose . . . things got a little out of hand.

Johnson tips his rocking chair forward and puts a hand on Wallace's knee.

Johnson I don't understand you, George, you used to be a real progressive New Dealer. Why are you off on this black thing? You ought to be back down there making sure Aunt Susie gets the help she needs in the nursing home.

Wallace I . . .

Johnson See, George, if you can stop harking back to 1865 and wake up to it being 1965, your President will help you! Think of the improvements you can make – for all races – in the Alabama education system. You got a lot of poor people down there, a lot of ignorant people. Listen, what do you want left after you when you die? You want a great big marble monument that reads: 'George Wallace – He Built'? Or you want a little bitty piece of scrawny pine board that reads: 'George Wallace – He Hated'?

He sits back triumphantly, resting his case. Wallace has no idea what to say. By a happy inspiration, Johnson now fetches Katzenbach's list out of his pocket and runs an eye over it.

You saw all those television cameras out there on your way in?

Wallace Yes.

Johnson Now, George, I know you love to be on television. Hell, I've watched you attacking me on television and you were so goddamn persuasive I had to turn off the set before you had me changing my mind about myself!

Wallace chuckles feebly.

I'm going to put something to you, something that'll turn off all these demonstrations in a heartbeat. Why don't you just desegregate all your schools? Then you and I can go out there right now in front of those cameras and you can announce it: 'I've decided to desegregate every school in Alabama.'

Silence. Wallace is gaping at him, appalled. Finally he manages to close his mouth.

Wallace You know I can't do that, Mr President. The schools are all locally run, they've got school boards. I don't have the power to make that kind of political decision.

Johnson OK, here's some other little suggestions.

He briefly consults his piece of paper. As he makes each point, he pauses long enough to register Wallace is not going to respond, before moving on.

You could undertake, in every circumstance, to obey all Federal Court orders.

You could commit to a guarantee of law enforcement without brutality, I thought we just agreed that was a good idea.

You could publicly support the right to peaceful assembly.

86

You could institute a series of meetings, biracial meetings, to discuss all your outstanding problems. No?

Wallace opens his mouth. Nothing comes out.

Well, all right, then, why don't you just come out with me and affirm the principle of universal suffrage?

Wallace Anybody who's registered in Alabama can vote.

Johnson Well, then we just say from now on, everybody in Alabama can be automatically registered, including nigras.

Wallace Mr President, under Alabama law, that power belongs to the county registrars. I don't have that power.

Johnson Now don't you shit me, George Wallace! Last year, unless I misremember, you had the power to keep the President of the United States off the Alabama ballot. And you're telling me you don't have the power to tell a few poor county registrars where they get off?

Wallace I . . . well, no, really, I don't.

Johnson rises to his feet.

Johnson So, I'm guessing you don't want to come out with me and make a joint statement.

Wallace I don't think I . . .

He's on his feet as well.

I really want to thank you for the opportunity to let me come here, Mr President.

Johnson takes him by the lapel and drapes his other arm over Wallace's shoulder.

Johnson Well, you just come on by whenever you feel like it, George.

Wallace Thank you, Mr President.

Johnson scoops up an ashtray from the coffee table.

Johnson And here's a little something for Lurleen, a souvenir from the White House.

Wallace Ah, thank you.

Johnson, by now, has him over to the door. He leans out, calling offstage.

Johnson The Governor needs to leave by the side entrance.

Wallace Well, I'm very . . .

But the door closes on him and he's gone. Johnson turns back into the room, grinning widely.

Johnson Great list, Nick.

Katzenbach I must say, Mr President, I'm impressed . . .

Johnson When I saw the little shit-heel wasn't going to give me anything, I thought least I could do was leave him with something to think about. Now . . .

Katzenbach Yes, sir?

Johnson I got another job for you, Nick.

Katzenbach Go ahead.

Johnson I'm going to go down and tell those fucking cameras I'm going to send the Voting Rights Bill to Congress next week.

Katzenbach But . . . ?

Johnson You're going to let me get that out, then you're going to interrupt me and say: 'Mr President, isn't this meant to be on background?' And I'm going to say: 'By God, yes, turn off those cameras.' But by then the damage will have been done, you get my meaning?

He shepherds Katzenbach out of the room.

NINE

15th March. A divided stage. Above, President Johnson addresses Congress and the nation. Below, in the modest living room of a house belonging to a Selma dentist, Sullivan Jackson, Martin Luther King and a number of his associates including John Lewis, twenty-five, chairman of the Student Non-Violent Coordinating Committee, whose head is still bandaged from Bloody Sunday, watch the speech on television. We can't see the screen, which faces upstage casting its bluish light: King sits in an armchair, close to the TV set. His associates react (as during King's eulogy) frequently, especially during the regular periods of applause in the Speaker's chambers.

Johnson At times history and fate meet at a single time in a single place to shape a turning point in man's unending search for freedom. So it was at Lexington and Concord. So it was a century ago at Appomattox. So it was last week in Selma, Alabama.

There, long-suffering men and women peacefully protested the denial of their rights as Americans. Many were brutally assaulted. One good man, a man of God, was killed.

John Lewis gives an indignant snort and speaks up.

Lewis He talks about Reeb, you notice he doesn't mention Jimmie Lee.

A general murmur of agreement in the room.

SNCC Man Yeah, he only cares about the white man.

King Give him a chance, John: and all of you, hush up.

All of these exchanges as Johnson is continuing to speak.

Johnson Rarely in any time does an issue lay bare the secret heart of America itself. The issue of equal rights for American Negroes is such an issue. And should we defeat every enemy, and should we double our wealth and conquer the stars and still be unequal to this issue, then we will have failed as a people and as a nation. For, with a country as with a person, 'What is a man profited if he shall gain the whole world and lose his own soul?'

A first round of applause; and now some positive reactions from those watching in Selma.

There is no Negro problem. There is no Southern problem. There is no Northern problem. There is only an American problem.

More applause. A real change of attitude now among the viewers in Selma.

Many of the issues of civil rights are very complex and most difficult. But about this there can and should be no argument: every American citizen must have an equal right to vote. Yet the harsh fact is that in many places in this country men and women are kept from voting simply because they are Negroes.

Every device of which human ingenuity is capable has been used to deny this right. No law that we now have on the books – and I have helped to put three of them there – can ensure the right to vote when local officials are determined to deny it. In such a case, our duty must be clear to all of us. The Constitution says that no person shall be kept from voting because of his race or his colour.

The last time a President sent a civil rights bill to the Congress it contained a provision to protect voting rights in Federal elections. That civil rights bill was passed after eight long months of debate. And when that bill came to my desk from the Congress for signature, the heart of the voting provision had been eliminated.

This time, on this issue, there must be no delay, no hesitation or no compromise with our purpose. We cannot, we must not, refuse to protect the right of every American to vote. We have already waited a hundred years and more and the time for waiting is gone.

A prolonged standing ovation in the chamber. In Selma, the spectators shift and look at one another.

Lewis My God, he sounds as if he means it.

Johnson But even if we pass this bill, the battle will not be over. What happened in Selma is part of a far larger movement which reaches into every section and state of America. It is the effort of American Negroes to secure for themselves the full blessings of American life. Their cause must be our cause too. Because it's not just Negroes, but really it's all of us, who must overcome the crippling legacy of bigotry and injustice.

And we shall overcome.

A shocked silence is followed by growing applause. In Selma, there's pandemonium, cheering and whooping. Only King is motionless, palpably moved.

SNCC Man Did he just say that?

Second Viewer Can you believe it?

Lewis is looking at King.

Lewis Are you all right, Martin?

King It's everything we asked for.

Lewis I've never seen you cry before.

King dabs at his eye as tears begin to spill.

Johnson It was more than a hundred years ago that Abraham Lincoln – a great president of another party – signed the Emancipation Proclamation. But emancipation

is a proclamation and not a fact. A century has passed –
more than a hundred years – and yet the Negro is not
equal. A century has passed since the day of promise and
the promise is unkept. The time of justice has now come,
and I tell you that I believe sincerely that no force can
hold it back. It is right in the eyes of man and God that
it should come, and when it does, I think that day will
brighten the lives of every American. For Negroes are not
the only victims.

My first job after college was as a teacher in Cotulla,
Texas, in a small Mexican-American school. Few of them
could speak English and I couldn't speak much Spanish.
My students were poor and they often came to class
without breakfast and hungry. And they knew even in
their youth the pain of prejudice. They never seemed to
know why people disliked them, but they knew it was so,
because I saw it in their eyes. And somehow you never
forget what poverty and hatred can do, when you see its
scars on the hopeful face of a young child.

I never thought then, in 1928, that I would be standing
here in 1965. It never even occurred to me in my fondest
dreams that I might have the chance to help the sons and
daughters of those students, and to help people like them
all over this country. But now I do have that chance.

And I'll let you in on a secret: I mean to use it.

*Another standing ovation in the Speaker's chambers.
By now, King is frankly weeping, mopping at his face
with a large white handkerchief.*

TEN

*Back in the Oval Office: President Johnson is in
conversation with his former mentor, Senator Richard
Russell of Georgia, the Chairman of the Senate Armed
Services Committee. He's a tall, almost bald man of sixty-*

seven, his back ramrod-straight, courtly and formal in manner (he was often compared to Robert E. Lee) and at the moment recuperating from an emergency operation brought on by his emphysema (which he always pronounces 'em-fy-see-muh'), which has left on his throat the fresh scar of a tracheotomy. He's nursing a Jack Daniel's, while Johnson is treating himself to a Cutty Sark and soda (the bottles stand on his desk). It's about noon.

Johnson What did I tell you? I told you not to go convalesce in Puerto Rico, it's so damp down there, rains every blessed afternoon. You need dry heat– what are those goddamn doctors thinking? I told you, you need to go to Palm Springs, I'll get you a nice house out there.

Russell I never will forget your thoughtfulness, I just wanted to tell you that.

Johnson Don't say that, Dick: since my momma and poppa got away from me, you're all I got left. I said more prayers about you than I have since Lady Bird threatened to divorce me . . .

Russell That's mighty sweet of you, Mr President.

Johnson Call me Lyndon, like you always used to.

Russell That was before you were the President.

Johnson Oh, come on! How's your nephew, how's poor little Bobby?

Russell He's bad; I don't think he's long for this world.

Johnson Don't say that, he's no more'n a boy!

Russell Yes, he's only forty, but that cancer, you know . . . Makes my emphysema look like a sore throat.

Johnson Where is he now?

Russell They got him up here in that National Institute of . . .

Johnson Health.

Russell Health, yes. Such a socialistic institution, they don't even let him buy an aspirin tablet.

Johnson We got the best doctors in the United States in Houston, you know. And we got a brand new plane parked in our barn up at the ranch, it's a honey, it can pick him up here and fly him right to Houston, there's a big bed on it, flies above the clouds and everything . . .

Russell says nothing. Silence. Johnson gets up and pours him another Jack Daniel's.

Did I break your heart?

Russell What do you mean?

Johnson With my Voting Rights Bill.

Russell Oh, no, I knew it was coming, sooner or later.

Johnson I heard tell you said I was a turncoat.

Russell We all say things in the heat of the moment.

Johnson Yes.

Russell Just I couldn't help remembering your maiden speech on the Senate floor. It was the backbone of our filibuster. I remember how you said you detested lynching, it was a shameful crime, but for the Federal Government to intervene and legislate directly against it would be an intolerable violation of the rights of the States, in favour of a wholly unnecessary law. You said the chasm of our differences would be irreparably widened. It was one of the ablest speeches I'd ever heard on the subject.

Johnson Why, thank you.

Russell Did you believe any of it?

Johnson I knew I needed to get on and move up and I believed that was the only way to do it.

Russell How right you were.

Johnson But I guess what I really believed was what I said the other night in Congress.

Russell These bills you're going to pass, Kennedy would never have got them through. We could have beaten John Kennedy on civil rights, but not you. You'll twist a man's arm off and beat his head in with it. You don't mind breaking all your old promises and antagonising all your old allies in the South, do you?

He sips his bourbon, watching Johnson consider his question.

Johnson I figured as long as I have the power, I should use it to do what I think is right. Otherwise what the hell's the presidency for?

Russell The chasm of our differences is vast, Mr President. But I don't see why that should affect our personal relationship.

Johnson Of course it shouldn't. I need you and I love you and there's lots of things I want you in besides civil rights. You made me and I know it and I don't ever forget. Matter of fact, if I had it my way, you'd be in my place.

Russell No, no, that would never do.

Johnson It would too. The country would be in a hell of a lot better shape.

Russell You're going to run it the next eight years. My emphysema's going to carry me off in two or three.

Johnson Now, don't you say that. Nobody ever has been more to me than you have, Dick, except my mother.

Russell gives a little snort of derisive laughter.

No, no, that's true. I just want to counsel with you and I want your judgement and your wisdom. And I'm going to have it.

Silence. Russell nods vestigially. Johnson looks away for a moment, then back to him.

What do you think of this Vietnam thing?

Russell raises his head and looks him straight in the eye.

Russell Frankly, Mr President, it's the damn worst mess I ever saw; and I don't like to brag. I never have been right many times in my life, but I knew we were going to get into this sort of mess when we went in there. You were there that last meeting we had with Eisenhower before we went in: I tried my best to stop them then, said we'd never get out, we'd still be there in fifty years' time.

Johnson I remember.

Russell And the position is deteriorating, isn't it? Looks like the more we try to do for them, the less they're willing to do for themselves. And now you've sent in the Marines.

Johnson Didn't have any choice. Sent in two battalions.

Russell Won't make a damn bit of difference. I tell you it's going to take a half-million men. And they'll be bogged down in there for ten years. And those Marines'll be killing a whole lot of friendly Vietnamese. We're going to wind up with the people we're trying to save being mad as hell with us. We're just like the damn cow over a fence out there. Course, if we'd had them hold free elections when we were getting into all this, they'd have voted for Ho Chi Minh and we wouldn't have a problem. What we need now is to get some fellow in there who *wants* us to get out. Then we'd have to abide by our theory of self-determination and go. But that's not going to happen.

Johnson No; in the meantime all anyone wants me to do is drop bombs. And that ain't worth a damn, Dick! I sent a hundred and sixty planes over to bomb a barracks: twenty-seven buildings and they set two of them on fire.

Russell Yeah, we tried it in Korea. We got a lot of B-29s and sent 'em over there and dropped millions and millions of bombs, they would knock out the road at night and in the morning, the damn people would be back travelling down it. And you ain't going to stop these people, either. Bombing them ain't worth a hoot.

Johnson I had McNamara on this morning recommending more strikes.

Russell McNamara's the smartest fellow that any of us know, but I'm not too sure he understands the history and the background of those people out there as fully as he should. He's got so damn opinionated, he's just plain made his mind up on all this.

Johnson I don't know what we can do; I don't see how we could move out.

Russell You could make a tremendous case for moving out.

Johnson But you got all the Senators, you got Nixon and Rockefeller and Goldwater all saying let's escalate the war, let's hit the North . . .

Russell Nixon, ha!

Johnson Now Nixon's a very capable guy: he's capable of ruining this entire country in eight years.

A wintry chuckle from Russell.

Thing is, if I walked out, they'd take Thailand and Cambodia and Burma, maybe even Indonesia and India, then I'd be another Chamberlain . . .

Russell Ah, the domino theory.

Johnson Well, yes.

Russell I think the domino theory's a lot of bull.

Johnson But a President who just ran out of there, they'd impeach him, wouldn't they?

Russell I doubt it.

Johnson I just don't see any way out of it.

Russell looks at him for a moment; then he speaks very quietly.

Russell Then what the hell's the presidency for?

Silence. Johnson's head sinks, he looks very shaken.

I'm sorry, Mr President. You couldn't have inherited a worse mess.

Johnson Well, if they say I inherited it, I'll be lucky. But they're all going to say I created it.

A light tap on the door and Jack Valenti shows in Lady Bird Johnson, but not before Johnson has swept the bottle of Cutty Sark and the glass into a drawer of his desk with practised skill and closed the drawer. Russell rises to his feet and Lady Bird hurries over to him and kisses him.

Lady Bird Oh, Senator . . .

Russell Hello, honey, how are you doing?

Lady Bird You just look a picture!

Russell A very dusty Old Master, maybe.

Lady Bird No, you look wonderful. I've come to bring you over to lunch.

Johnson We got a good hamburger for you, the way you like it.

Lady Bird You're like us, Senator, you got a-plenty ahead of you, so you're just going to have to recuperate your strength and get back at it!

Russell Whatever you say, ma'am.

Lady Bird Let's go, shall we?

Johnson Take Dick, will you, Bird, I just need a few minutes with Jack.

Lady Bird You make sure it is a few minutes, we're not waiting on you . . .

Johnson Sure, sure, two minutes, darlin'.

Lady Bird leads Russell out of the room. Valenti waits. Eventually Johnson turns to him, frowning.

Valenti What can I do for you, Mr President?

Johnson Damn if I haven't forgotten what I wanted to say to you.

He concentrates vainly for a moment.

Fuck!

Valenti Are you all right, Mr President?

Johnson I've had a little bit of a shock, Jack. Man I respect most in the world telling me I ought to get out of Vietnam. What do you think of that?

Valenti Everyone's entitled to their opinion, sir, but from my perspective, you're handling the Vietnam problem just brilliantly.

Johnson He said it was going to take a half-million men and ten years.

Valenti Well, that's ridiculous. He's been ill, hasn't he?

Johnson Yeah, he's ill.

Valenti Has he never married?

Johnson He had a sweetheart once, long time ago, but she was a Catholic and he thought it would be wrong to marry her. But he kept the flame burning and never thought of marrying anyone else. That's the kind of man he is.

Valenti Belongs to a vanished world, Mr President. I'm sure that's why he doesn't have any idea what the right way forward might be in Vietnam.

Johnson ignores this completely. He turns to Valenti, his expression fierce.

Johnson Want to know why we're in Vietnam?

Valenti Ah, why, Mr President?

Johnson unzips his fly and brings out what is evidently a substantial member.

Johnson This.

Valenti, alarmed, has taken an involuntary step back.

This is why.

He tucks himself away.

We got it all the way in and now we don't have the heart to take it out.

He zips up his pants, sighs.

I got to speak to that tailor. He never makes the crotch deep enough, so it cuts under my nuts all the way to my bumhole.

He shakes his head, pensive.

I tell you, Jack, that Vietnam's going to be the death of me.

ELEVEN

25th March. Martin Luther King stands on a flatbed truck at the foot of the steps leading up to the Capitol building in Montgomery, Alabama, addressing a crowd of more than 25,000 people. As before, we see only the small group closest to him, below, which includes John Lewis and Coretta Scott King, thirty-seven, handsome and elegant. Again, King's speech is punctuated with cries of empathy and encouragement from the crowd.

King Last Sunday, more than eight thousand of us started on a mighty walk from Selma, Alabama. They told us we wouldn't get here. There were those who told us we would get here only over their dead bodies, but all the world today knows that we are here and we are standing before the forces of power in the state of Alabama saying: 'We ain't goin' let nobody turn us around.'

Now, it is not an accident that one of the great marches of American history should terminate in Montgomery, Alabama. Just ten years ago, in this very city, a new philosophy was born of the Negro struggle. Out of this struggle, more than bus desegregation was won; a new idea, more powerful than guns or clubs, was born. The method of non-violent resistance was unsheathed from its scabbard and an entire community was mobilised to confront the adversary. And so Selma, Alabama has become a shining moment in the conscience of man. If the worst in American life lurked in its dark streets, the best of American instincts arose passionately from across the nation to overcome it. There never was a moment in American history more honourable and more inspiring than the pilgrimage of clergymen and laymen of every race and faith pouring into Selma to face danger at the side of its embattled Negroes.

The confrontation of good and evil compressed in the tiny community of Selma generated the massive power to turn the whole nation to a new course. A president born in the South had the sensitivity to feel the will of the country and, in an address that will live in history as one of the most passionate pleas for human rights ever made by a president of our nation, he pledged the might of the Federal Government to cast off the centuries-old blight. President Johnson rightly praised the courage of the Negro for awakening the conscience of the nation.

On our part we must pay our profound respect to the white Americans who cherish their democratic traditions over the ugly customs and privileges of generations and come forth boldly to join hands with us. And I stand before you this afternoon with the conviction that segregation is on its deathbed in Alabama, and the only thing uncertain about it is how costly the segregationists and Wallace will make the funeral.

Our whole campaign in Alabama has been centred around the right to vote. And the battle is in our hands. The battle is in our hands in Mississippi and Alabama and all over the United States. I know there is a cry today in Alabama, we see it in numerous editorials: 'When will Martin Luther King and all of these civil rights agitators and all of the white clergymen and labour leaders and students and others get out of our community and let Alabama return to normalcy?'

I have a message that I would like to leave with Alabama this evening. It was normalcy in Mississippi that led to the killing of three civil rights workers last summer; it was normalcy in Marion that led to the brutal murder of Jimmie Lee Jackson; it was normalcy in Birmingham that led to the murder on a Sunday morning of four, beautiful, unoffending, innocent girls; it was normalcy on Highway 80 that led State Troopers to use tear gas and horses and billy clubs against unarmed human beings who were simply marching for justice; it was normalcy by a café in Selma, Alabama, that led to the brutal beating of Reverend James Reeb.

It is normalcy all over our country which leaves the Negro perishing on a lonely island of poverty in the midst of a vast ocean of material prosperity. It is normalcy all over Alabama that prevents the Negro from becoming a registered voter. No, we will not allow Alabama to return to normalcy.

The only normalcy that we will settle for is the normalcy of brotherhood, the normalcy of true peace, the normalcy of justice. The end we seek is a society that can live with its conscience. And that will be a day not of the white man, not of the black man. That will be the day of man as man.

I know you are asking today: 'How long will it take?' 'How long will justice be crucified and truth bear it?'

I come to say to you this afternoon, however difficult the moment, however frustrating the hour, it will not be long, because truth crushed to earth will rise again.

How long? Not long, because no lie can live for ever.

How long? Not long, because you shall reap what you sow.

How long? Not long, because the arc of the moral universe is long, but it bends toward justice.

How long? Not long, because:

Mine eyes have seen the glory of the coming of the Lord;
He is trampling out the vintage where the grapes of
    wrath are stored;

He has loosed the fateful lightning of his terrible
    swift sword;
His truth is marching on.

He has sounded forth the trumpet that shall never
    call retreat;
He is sifting out the hearts of men before his judgement
    seat.
O, be swift my soul to answer him! Be jubilant, my
    feet!
Our God is marching on.

Glory, hallelujah! Glory, hallelujah!
Glory, hallelujah! Glory, hallelujah!
His truth is marching on.

*Massive applause. Eventually, King steps down and
embraces Coretta. Lewis, a small white bandage still
protecting his skull, shakes hands with him.*

Hard-hitting enough for you, John?

Lewis It was a great speech, Martin.

King Thank you, but I'm afraid a lot of your people are
going to say: too little, too late. You're going to be
needing to watch your back.

Coretta Look at all the Church people here, Martin. This
just may be the greatest witness since the days of the
early Christians.

King Let's not exaggerate . . .

Coretta Daddy just said to me: 'This is the greatest day
for Negroes in the history of America.'

King I improvised a little at the end there, was that OK?

Coretta Superb. I'm just so sorry I didn't bring the
children, I should have . . .

She's interrupted by the arrival of an attractive redhead of thirty-nine, Viola Liuzzo, who stretches out her hand to a rather surprised King.

Vi Dr King, I just wanted to say to you, I'll never forget that speech, as long as I live.

King Well, thank you . . .

Vi My name's Vi Liuzzo, I drove down from Detroit to do whatever I could to help out.

King That's a long drive.

Vi Soon as I saw those television pictures from Selma, I thought I had to come down and volunteer and do anything I could to make myself useful.

King So what have you . . .?

Vi Oh, driving between here and Selma with anyone who needs a ride, picking people up from the airport, helping out at the first-aid station, you know, putting Band-Aids on blisters, handing out lotion for sunburn.

King Well, we couldn't have done what we've done without people like you.

Vi My husband's a Teamster: he said, go do what you have to, I'll look after the kids.

King How many do you have?

Vi Five.

King One better than us. This is Mrs King, by the way.

Vi and Coretta shake hands, Coretta with some reserve. For a moment it seems as if Vi is going to move away: then she turns back to King.

Vi I hope you don't mind, I wanted to . . .

King What?

Vi Please don't think I'm crazy. I'm kind of noted for this, all my friends and family will tell you: I have premonitions.

King Really.

Vi Yes, and this morning I had the strongest premonition ever. Of evil. It was like an anxiety attack, I was having trouble breathing. And I said to this Irish priest I was with, Father Deasy, I said, I feel as sure as can be someone's going to be killed today.

King Well, we get threats, death threats most every day, Mrs . . .

Vi Liuzzo.

King Mrs Liuzzo, we're used to them. We just try to put them out of our minds.

Vi It wasn't you, Dr King, it wasn't you I thought was going to be killed: in fact, the person who came into my head was Governor Wallace. Seemed to me somebody might kill him, so the marchers would get blamed . . .

King I don't think you need to worry your head about that, Mrs Liuzzo. George Wallace isn't going to show his face any time today, I can guarantee you of that.

Coretta We need to be moving along, Mrs Liuzzo.

Vi Of course, yes, I'm sorry, I just thought . . .

King We appreciate all your help and concern, Mrs Liuzzo. Try not to worry. And we are really grateful to you, like I said, we couldn't go on without people like you.

Vi Thank you, Dr King, that means the world to me . . .

King shakes her hand warmly and she slips back into the crowd. Coretta watches her go, troubled.

Coretta Have you met her before?

King No. I don't think so. No. Why?

Coretta looks away for a moment, hesitating: then she decides to go ahead.

Coretta I didn't want to tell you before your speech, but the office in Atlanta passed a package along to me.

King A package?

Coretta A tape.

All of a sudden, she has his complete attention.

They passed it along to me, because they thought it was one of your speeches, so they . . . passed it along to me for my archive.

King Yes?

Coretta It was posted from Miami. No one noticed there was a letter with it, a kind of a letter, anonymous, really sick and disgusting, one of the worst I've seen . . .

King And the tape? What was on the tape?

She looks at him for a long moment. He's terrified. She makes a clear decision.

Coretta I don't know. I couldn't tell. Strange noises. Really just a lot of mumbo-jumbo. You better listen to it when you get back to Atlanta.

King Yes.

Coretta Are we going back tonight?

King Well . . . I don't know . . .

Coretta I think we should. We have to make a decision on that house. We have less than a week.

King I don't see why we have to own a house, Coretta. What's wrong with renting?

Coretta Listen, I knew you were going to give all the Nobel money away, I completely respect that decision, I know you as good as paid for this entire march out of your own pocket: but it really is time we had somewhere of our own.

King But it's such a big house. And ten thousand dollars . . .

Coretta It isn't so big. And we have four growing children. They need somewhere to play. A garden. You're away all the time. We need somewhere to be; I need it, if you're going to spend so much time . . . away.

They look at each other. Eventually, King lowers his head.

King You're right. You deserve it. It's the least I can do.

TWELVE

26th March. President Johnson sits behind his desk in the Oval Office looking out at Katzenbach, Valenti, J. Edgar Hoover and Cartha DeLoach. It's around noon.

Johnson Well, you're a miracle-worker, Edgar. It's nothing less than a goddamn miracle.

Hoover Thank you, Mr President.

Johnson I'm just sorry we had to keep you waiting all morning, but what with the Medicare Bill and . . . the fuckin' astronauts . . .

Hoover That's all right, I understand your schedule is . . .

Johnson But don't you worry, I'm going to give you your due at the Press Conference, I'm going to say . . . matter of fact, I'll tell you exactly what I'm going to say . . .

He reaches for some sheets of paper on his desk and reads from one of them.

I'm going to say: 'I cannot express myself too strongly in praising Mr Hoover and the men of the FBI for their prompt and expeditious performance in handling this investigation.'

Hoover Well, that is very gratifying, Mr President.

Johnson No more'n you deserve. I mean, to make an arrest inside twelve hours!

Hoover says nothing. Johnson turns to Valenti.

Reminds me, I got to find out how to pronounce this woman's name, have to ask my resident Eyetalian. Jack?

Valenti Liuzzo.

Johnson Liuzzo.

He makes a pretty good hash of the name; then he turns back to Hoover.

Like I said, to make an arrest inside twelve hours. How'd you do it?

Hoover's uncomfortable, but Johnson's tone has suddenly changed to something sharp and penetrating. Hoover exchanges a glance with DeLoach, who immediately looks extremely anxious. Then Hoover takes a deep breath and bites the bullet.

Hoover We had one of our men in the car.

Johnson In her car?

Hoover No, no, in the Klan car. She was giving a ride to a black kid and the Klan car overtook her and fired about ten or twelve shots at her through the window. Pretty much blew her head off. The boy was lucky, didn't even get a scratch. Our man didn't have a gun, of course, he didn't do any shooting; but, as soon as he could, he came in and he identified the two shooters.

Johnson So you . . . infiltrated the KKK?

Hoover If you remember, Mr President, we had a conversation last year, right before the Fourth of July, and you said we ought to get after the Klan, just as if they were Communists. You said you didn't want them to order a pizza without us knowing about it. And I took you at your word.

Johnson You hired people to join the Klan?

Hoover No, we went to some people already in the Klan and persuaded them to give us information. We pay them. Sometimes they demand a pretty high price. For instance, those three bodies we were looking for in Mississippi, we had to pay thirty thousand dollars, just to find the location. Anyway, this man, our informant, fortunately just happened to be in on this thing last night. Otherwise we'd be looking for a needle in a haystack.

Johnson I see. Now, the husband of this Miz . . .

He snaps his fingers.

Valenti Liuzzo.

Johnson Liuzzo, he's been calling the White House all morning. See any reason why I shouldn't get back to him?

Hoover Well, I wouldn't rush to do that if I were you, Mr President. See, when I said she was giving this black boy a ride, I wasn't kidding . . .

DeLoach sniggers, slightly annoying Hoover.

He was tucked right up beside her, they were sitting very, very close, the whole thing had all the appearances of a necking party. And I think we're going to see narcotics being involved. They found, uh, they found on her body numerous needle points indicating she may have been taking dope.

Johnson Is that so?

Hoover And the husband, uh, he's a Teamster, I don't say he's a bad character, but he's well known in Detroit as being one of the Teamsters' strong-arm men. So I'd be somewhat inclined to have someone else call him.

Johnson I see, thank you.

He broods for a moment, concealing his distaste; then recovers, with a jolt of energy.

Wonderful job, Edgar, thank you.

Hoover receives the compliment with a gracious smile.

DeLoach The Director even got a congratulatory telegram from Martin Luther King.

Johnson He did?

Hoover I don't intend to dignify it with a reply.

DeLoach I don't think he'd have sent it if he knew what we just did.

Johnson Oh, what was that?

Hoover shoots DeLoach a warning glance, but he's already launched.

DeLoach We sent him a gift from Miami: a tape our boys had cut together of some of his most impressive endeavours in the hotels and motels of America. His greatest hits.

Hoover That's enough, Deke.

DeLoach I'm sorry, Director.

Johnson Well, Edgar, we're on TV in ten, Jack will take you down. I just need a minute with Nick.

They're all on their feet, and Valenti ushers Hoover and DeLoach out of the room. Johnson waits till the door closes behind them, then turns to Katzenbach.

I have nothing to say to you, Nick; I just needed to get that slippery old fart out the door.

Katzenbach I completely understand.

Johnson What the hell was all that about? That poor woman had five kids, drove the family car all the way to Selma, Alabama to help out, she's like a cut-out model of a well-meaning liberal idealist; and he's talking about drugs and necking with black kids. What planet is he from?

Katzenbach And her husband, I talked to him already, he's really in control of himself, sounded like a pretty fine fellow to me. Tony Liuzzo. You should call him.

Johnson I will, of course I will. Now I know he's not an enforcer for the Teamsters.

Katzenbach You're right, what the hell is Hoover up to?

Johnson I'll tell you what I think. Ol' Edgar's scared somebody's going to say if there was an FBI guy in the killers' car, why didn't he call it in *before* they murdered that poor woman? If he makes everyone think she was a niggerlovin' junkie, it'll maybe distract them from asking the question and he comes up smelling of roses.

Katzenbach Well, it's certainly worked so far. You see what they said in the *New York Times*, no less?

He picks up a copy of the Times *from the desk, reads aloud.*

'J. Edgar Hoover is an authentic American folk hero, the incorruptible idol of generations of American youngsters and the symbol of the "honest cop" to millions of their elders.'

Johnson The *New York Times*, huh?

Katzenbach The *New York Times*.

Johnson Poor bastards, what do they know? Nobody's going to tell them there was an informant in the car, they're going to go right on thinking Edgar can walk on water. And what a day for them, huh? Have we ever had three televised press conferences before lunch? Must be the biggest news day since Columbus got his feet wet and moseyed up the beach.

He starts gathering together his papers.

Katzenbach I must say, the Medicare broadcast was a triumph. The way you handled Senator Byrd . . .

Johnson Yeah, I squeezed old Harry's balls good, didn't I? Got him to say on camera that he'd hurry the vote along in committee. On camera! So he can't welsh like that little shit Wallace making me have to federalise the Alabama National Guard all over again. We're going to get that Medicare Bill through, Nick! And then the . . .

Katzenbach Astronauts.

Johnson The fuckin' astronauts, yeah, how can you go wrong with an astronaut? And now this goddamn old pterodactyl. Just shows what a deep hole we're in, doesn't it, Nick?

Katzenbach What does, Mr President?

Johnson This country's senior law enforcement officer is a seventy-year-old, unfirable, mean, bigoted, blackmailing, paranoid, unregenerate son of a bitch, who believes there's no such thing as organised crime: and he's the least of my problems!

He puts his arm round Katzenbach's shoulders and steers him out of the room.

THIRTEEN

It's winter 2010. Sitting behind a plain table in the bare, bleak interview room of a state prison in Alabama is an old man: James Bonard Fowler, now seventy-six, alone, waiting. A door clangs open and a black Prison Guard wheels in a wheelchair containing a bald, bespectacled man, over eighty years old, but with eyes alive and sparkling with malice. This is Edgar Ray Killen, convicted in 2005 for organising the murders of the Civil Rights workers James Chaney, Andrew Goodman and Mickey Schwerner in Neshoba County, Mississippi. Fowler rises to his feet to shake hands with Killen, who then motions the Guard to install him alongside the table.

Killen Trooper Fowler.

Fowler Mr Killen.

In position now, Killen looks up at the Guard.

Killen Thank you, boy. They told you you could leave us alone, didn't they?

The Guard nods, his expression surly. He leaves the room and Killen turns back to Fowler, beaming.

Well, it's an honour to meet you, sir.

Fowler I couldn't believe it when they told me about this. I thought you were still . . .

Killen That's right, only four years into a sixty-year sentence in Rankin County jail. But, you know, I still got a few friends able to set me up a little Christmas treat.

Fowler I'm impressed.

Killen But they only gave you six months, am I right?

Fowler Yes, sir: plea bargain. The DA, only black DA they got in Alabama, he knew no jury would convict me . . .

Killen See, that's where Alabama's still got it over Mississippi. I read the other day where some nigger in Selma just got two hundred years for robbing a garage and shooting the owner.

Fowler Two hundred years?

Killen Good behaviour, he'll be out in fifty.

They laugh.

Yeah, so, he got two hundred years, you got six months: see what I'm saying about Alabama?

Fowler I do.

Killen And plea bargain, you were telling me?

Fowler Part of the deal was, he made me apologise in court to the family. I had to do it, but, you know, I made sure I didn't look at them.

Killen This nigger DA you're talking about?

Fowler That's right.

Killen You know, I remember saying fifty years ago, if they bring in this goddamn Voting Rights Bill, next thing you know, there'll be a nigger in the White House.

They both contemplate this for a moment, their expressions solemn.

Anyway, six months ain't so bad.

Fowler Yeah, I did longer than that in a jail in Thailand, but that's another story.

Killen Tell them you're ill, they'll let you out sooner. I made an appeal bond that way, coulda been all right, but that fuckin' judge, I think someone musta been blackmailing him, I caught a real bad break.

Fowler Luck of the draw.

Killen Anyway, I wanted to know, when you killed that nigger . . . can't recall his name, now . . .

Fowler Jimmie Lee Jackson.

Killen Jackson, yeah: were you chastised at the time? Were you disciplined?

Fowler Nope. I was promoted. Transferred and promoted.

Killen Then you killed another nigger the following year, is that right?

Fowler Yeah. Also self-defence.

Killen Well, yes, of course, that goes without saying. And did you get into trouble that second time?

Fowler Not for a minute. Only trouble I got into, I had a fight with my supervisor and pushed his face through the windshield of his cruiser. Cost me my badge.

Killen Tough.

Fowler No, it was all right, I went to Vietnam. My brother got killed out there, so I went out and offed as many gooks as I could find.

Killen Point I'm making is, you didn't get in no trouble for the niggers?

Fowler Not then, no.

Killen Then how'd you wind up here?

Fowler Talked to a journalist.

Killen That's always a big mistake.

Fowler You said it. I just, you know, told him what happened. I thought, hell, it's been forty-five years, nobody's said a word, I figured there must be some kind of . . . statute of limitations.

Killen Well, sure, of course. Listen, when I was a kid in Mississippi, I had no idea it was against the law to kill a nigger. Guy who told me, I thought he was joking with me.

Fowler nods in complete agreement.

Fowler And all these assholes keep telling me I'm a racist. That's so stupid, I'm not a racist! I think Nelson Mandela is a great man. Hell, my wife is Burmese.

Killen They'll never get within a mile of understanding the way we think. I'm a man of God.

Pause. He settles in his wheelchair.

Most everyone thinks well of me; I been a jackleg preacher all my life. I pastored churches all over Neshoba County for more than fifty years. But I'm like you, you know, I'm a good soldier, I follow orders. Anyways, back in the summer of nineteen hundred and sixty-four, which was a hot one, I get a call from the Imperial Wizard and he issues me with an order number four, you understand what I'm saying? He tells me there's these three troublemakers come down from up North, a Commie and a Jewboy and a nigger, Civil Rights workers, scum of the earth; and he says he wants their rear ends tore up.

So I call my guys, I just have to say two words: payday's comin'. First thing, I had the deputies arrest them and throw them in Neshoba County jail, so I could buy me a little time, enough to figure out a plan. I had the big dozer moved over to the dam and working; and late in the evening we released them. They beat up on the nigger a little too heavy with them chains, which wasn't too smart, because he was the driver, but turned out he was still able to drive. They cut them off out on Highway 19 and rode their asses down to Rock Cut Road. Wayne Roberts took the Jew out of the patrol car. You know what he said? Wayne asked him if he was a niggerlover and he said, 'Sir, I know just how you feel.'

How do you like that? Wayne shot him, then he executed the Commie. Jimmy Jordan was pissed. He said: 'You didn't leave me nothing but a nigger.' Then he shot him anyway and said, 'Well, at least I killed me a nigger.' They took the bodies over to the dam and dug 'em in with the dozer, down where the sun don't shine, in fifteen feet of Mississippi clay. They'd never have been found, 'cept some greedy fuck squealed to the FBI for cash.

A job well done, wouldn't you say? We didn't get no more trouble out of them.

It was Father's Day, as I recall. But that's OK. The nigger was the only one with children.

Long silence.

Well, my friend. Just wanted you to know someone was looking out for you.

Totally unexpectedly, he rises to his feet.

Got some more calls to make.

He ambles comfortably over to the door and calls out.

Boy!

He walks back towards Fowler, hand extended, and shakes hands with him.

Takes more'n they know to put a good man down, am I right?

Fowler nods, says nothing. The Guard has returned and now Killen moves back towards the door, leaving the Guard to push the empty wheelchair behind him. Killen turns in the doorway, letting the Guard go past him.

Keep fighting the good fight, y'hear?

He leaves. Fowler sits at the table, motionless, looking out front as the light slowly fades.